THE

MOTLEY FOOL'S
MONEY AFTER 40

Building Wealth for a Better Life

DAVID AND TOM GARDNER

A FIRESIDE BOOK
Published by Simon & Schuster
New York   London   Toronto   Sydney

FIRESIDE
Rockefeller Center
1230 Avenue of the Americas
New York, NY 10020

This Fireside Edition 2006

FIRESIDE and colophon are registered trademarks of Simon & Schuster, Inc.

The Motley Fool, Fool, and the Jester logo are registered trademarks
of The Motley Fool, Inc.

For information about special discounts for bulk purchases,please contact
Simon & Schuster Special Sales at 1-800-456-6798 or business@simonandschuster.com.

Designed by Katy Riegel

Manufactured in the United States of America

5   7   9   10   8   6   4

The Library of Congress has cataloged the hardcover edition as follows:

Gardner, David, date.
The Motley Fool's money after 40 : building wealth for a better life /
David and Tom Gardner.
p.   cm.
Includes index.
1. Finance, Personal.   2. Investments.   I. Gardner, Tom, date.   II. Title.
HG179.G3175   2004
332.024'01'0844—dc22   2003067352

ISBN-13: 978-0-7432-2999-9
ISBN-10:   0-7432-2999-1
ISBN-13: 978-0-7432-8482-0 (Pbk)
ISBN-10:   0-7432-8482-8 (Pbk)

The authors and publisher gratefully acknowledge permission
from the following source:

Excerpt from "The Truly Great" by Stephen Spender, copyright © by
Stephen Spender, from *Selected Poems* by Stephen Spender.
Used by permission of Random House, Inc.

To the 394 venturesome people who, with royal good taste and the foresight of Tiresias, first subscribed to our fledgling Motley Fool newsletter, *pre-Fool.com*, more than ten years ago. You know who you are (drop us an email to say hi!), and we thank you again for the jolt of electricity that you gave to Foolishness.

Contents

PART THREE
HAVING MORE THAN ENOUGH

PART FOUR
HAVING IT ALL

Foreword

What to Expect, in 250 Words

 PLEASED TO MAKE your acquaintance. You have in your hands *a colorful and concise companion for your money* through the latter decades of your life.

We're David and Tom Gardner, authors of a wide range of books on money and investing, none of which—until this—was specifically written for Americans forty and older. Before we begin our journey together to map your finances, we want you to expect three things.

First, *expect plain English.* That's trademark Motley Foolish. We won't be flinging jargon at you. You shouldn't ever have to duck.

Second, *expect utility.* Our topics matter. Tied to them are such dollar amounts, such potential tension, and—yes—even possibly such eventual happiness that if we do our job well, the price of this book will seem nothing by comparison. To paraphrase Shakespeare's *Henry V* (Act IV, Scene III):

> *And gentlefolk in America, now a-bed,*
> *Shall think themselves accurs'd they missed this book;*
> *And hold retirement cheap whiles any speaks*
> *That browsed with us these leaves upon Saint Crispin's day.*
> *(Or any other day, for that matter.)*

Finally, *expect fun.* You cringe: "Fun reading about medical insurance?" You're darn tootin'! Our charge is to ring sugar around the medicine, as it were, en route to your completing tasks critical to your liberation from financial worry. And amusement fuels intellectual curiosity! It is therefore our solemn pledge to keep you learning, smiling, and profiting the whole way through.

Plain English, utility, fun. Proceed.

Introduction

May We Help You?

Everybody needs money! That's why they call it "money"!
—DAVID MAMET

 IT WAS THE summer of 1994. The stock market was falling, talk of recession was in the air. The Internet was rising out of its niche into the mass market. And we decided to put everything professional on hold in order to transform our modest newsletter, "The Motley Fool" into a business. We had no anticipation of success. No plan to work together full time for the next ten years (had we known, things would be different). It was a sweltering summer in the nation's capital. We swept out the shed on the back of David's property, sat two computers side to side on rickety card tables, balanced Fool caps on our monitors, drank ginger ales, and set ourselves to the task of fielding financial questions online.

Should I buy stock in Intel?

What can I do to keep from getting rooked by a car dealer?

How can I teach my children about money?

What's the difference between fixed-rate and adjustable-rate mortgages?

Is my broker taking advantage of me?

What should I do if I have $9,000 of credit-card debt?

Is it a good idea to buy the annuity my advisor is selling?

Should I part with my shares of Xerox?

When is it best to take my Social Security distributions, at sixty-two or sixty-five?

The last decade has thrown a flood of financial inquiries our way. There were times when the flood was so ceaseless that our email boxes could've been declared Superfund sites. All the while our harmless little acorn venture, watered by your curiosity, was blossoming into an oak tree.

Two years later, we signed our first book deal with Simon & Schuster, the firm that's published our more than half-dozen books. Right about when the media started asking if the Brothers Fool could possibly be serious, we signed on to syndicate a column of financial education into the business sections of the nation's newspapers.

Public demand for education about finance was on the upswing.

And why not?

Seventy-five million baby boomers were heading into the second half of their lives.

We then cobbled together our profits and built our own studio at Fool Global Headquarters in Alexandria, Virginia, where each week we broadcast The Motley Fool radio show for NPR. A study by market analyst Fallon Research concluded that one out of every four Internet users has visited The Motley Fool at Fool.com and that millions of people encounter The Fool each month.

Why the heck do you care about any of that?

Well, because you might be surprised to hear who it is we've been serving all these years.

Has it been college students or newcomers to the workforce—anyone or anything approaching a potential date for thirty-six-year-old bachelor Tom Gardner? No. Even though we staunchly believe the best time to begin retirement planning is *when you're twenty-one* (it's a lifelong plan and pursuit), and even though we hope you'll share portions of this book with your kids, alas, our audience isn't markedly green. The occasional nineteen-year-old does come to one of our book signings, and we always draw everyone's attention to these forward-thinking young people and point out that by starting early, they—in the words of the subtitle of our *Motley Fool Investment Guide for Teens*—will likely obtain "more money than their parents ever dreamed of." But these devotees are few and far between.

So who are you all?

More than 80 percent of our audience is over the age of forty-five. Half men, half women. And only the smallest minority of you received a formal financial education. At book signings, conferences, and events, we've addressed primarily people like you, people treading either side of the half-century mark with questions about how to have enough cash to:

- Live a comfortable life
- Provide fuel to worthy charities
- Pay for your kids to head off to summer camp (out-of-doors *without* PlayStation)
- Build your bridge to a second career
- Take care of your parents
- Bond with Jimmy Buffett in Margaritaville

In your hands, you hold the knowledge we've gained and shared with the many millions society has stuffed into a category called "baby boomers." Just about 25 percent of our nation's population fits into what sometimes seems an utterly useless classification: boomers. After all, you're everything under the sun. You're the most astonishing blend of diversity ever assembled in one place, under one flag. While you almost unanimously support individual, social, political, spiritual, and economic freedom, you share loads of distinguishing features.

So how do we speak to all of you individually at once?

Some of you are tall, some are reckless, some are poets, some own cats, some research individual stocks, some search the sky for meaning, some sleep late on Sundays, some prefer alternative healing, some love reading, some have recovered from cancer, some chew bubble gum, some run marathons, some find life absurd, and some would do anything imaginable not to read a book on financial planning for retirement.

But the great majority of you share one common trait.

We've said it once. We'll do so again.

What you know about money, you've learned yourself, often through trial and error. Damn that whole-life insurance package.

And curse those penny stocks a broker sold you over the phone. But you've learned. All in all, you've done extraordinarily well. But do you have enough to ensure the freedom you'll covet from age sixty onward?

Our book's aim is to help you answer yes, but only if yes *is* the answer. For ten years now, we've worked with you boomers (we promise to avoid that trite word as much as possible) to draw up financial plans sturdy enough to transport dreams: a second home somewhere along the Pacific Ocean. Time to volunteer in the community. Sufficient health-care coverage. A chance to throw a little magic into the lives of grandchildren. A combination cruise-train-RV-jetpack-mountain-bike-airplane journey around the world. Enough dough to cover alimony payments and pay for your third husband's head of new hair.

The resources to turn a hobby into a small business.

Spare change.

The good life.

FOR FURTHER THINKING

Whether building a financial plan or starting a business, you need to surround yourself with good people. Famous Wally Amos did just that:

David: How'd you start Famous Amos Cookies?

Wally Amos: In Hollywood, California, 1975. Opened the first store to ever sell chocolate chip cookies. It started with just an idea—as everything starts, with just an idea—and I got a group of friends together who supported it. Helen Reddy and Jeff Wall were initial investors. Marvin Gaye was one of the initial investors. I started with an investment of $25,000.

Tom: This was your Dream Team.

Amos: It *was* my Dream Team. No question about it. But you know what I discovered also is that they believed in me. They did not invest in an idea. I think people invest in other people, not in ideas.

Yes, the whole purpose of this book is to secure for you just that: the good life. Our book is laid out in four simply titled sections:

I. Get Ready
II. Having Enough
III. Having More Than Enough
IV. Having It All

This book is about gathering the resources to *have it all*. Veteran Fools know all this demands capital. But we aren't money-obsessed, and we don't wear blinders to the nonmonetary beauties of life. Having it all does not merely mean having a ton of cash. Not everyone has figured that out; a den of thieves in corporate America pilfered the system at the turn of this century for massive financial gain. They have enough. In a financial sense, they have *more* than enough; they're loaded. They'll ski the Matterhorn. Body-surf the Caribbean. Lie down in soft silk sheets. And rise to servants offering Egg Beaters, wheat toast, fresh strawberries, and a tall glass of freshly squeezed orange juice any day they darn well please.

But is that really having it all?

It may seem like it at times. On the surface, it is.

But what's always been missing in such people is any appreciation or understanding of the relative values of those things that can never be bought. Honor, self-respect, integrity, goodness—things worth more than any silk sheet or served entrée. You don't need to settle for either financial security or a meaningful life. You should have both.

Every one of us, no matter where we are today—in fact, no matter what we've done—has a shot at claiming financial security *and* a soul. You may be forty-nine years old, with $14,000 in credit-card debt, an oversize mortgage, a stock portfolio that collapsed, a child in and out of reform school, and no job stability. Or you may be a retired telecom executive who skimmed $20 million out of your business before it went under. Yes, you, too, can have security *and* a soul. (Our first recommendation—get down to the business of giving lots and lots away.)

Most of us are somewhere in between those extremes. The challenge is to continue or to get started in the right direction. For a

Fool, life is always more about future direction than present location.

So what lies ahead for you in these pages?

A flurry of opportunity, an integration of philosophy, a chance to learn.

In "Having Enough," we'll help you organize your finances, save more cash, cover your health-insurance needs, build a suitable investment portfolio, and calculate what capital you'll need for the next few decades. In "Having More Than Enough," we'll unravel Social Security, paying for your children to attend college, caring for your parents, and strengthening your investment portfolio. In the final section, "Having It All," we'll provide detailed advice on how to squash people en route to becoming a powerhouse corporate executive, how to fraudulently design shell corporations, how to cajole auditors into crooked accounting, and how to siphon shareholder money into offshore accounts.

Or not.

In truth, our final section will set you up to live a healthy, productive life—one with hobbies, an adventure or two, and even a second or third career.

We admit that the decision to put a given chapter in a given section of a book is by no means clear-cut. Many might argue, for instance, that "What to Do with Your Parents" is a necessity, and therefore is about having enough, not having more than enough. In our experience, continuing and eventually ending (at death) your relationship with your parents—done really right—is something many people unfortunately can't optimize, due to other limitations or demands on their time, geography, or limited resources. That's why we think of it as having—or, in this case, *doing*—more than enough. As the philosopher says, "Your mileage may vary." Of course, we hope you'll read the whole book and, where necessary, cut us a little slack if our ideas of what is average and what is above average don't conform perfectly to your own notions. As we said above: This book truly is about helping you where you need to be helped, regardless of what level of affluence or freedom you enjoy or aspire to.

We believe that in our own ways, on our own terms, every single one of us can *have it all* from here, no matter how prolonged or brief our stay. Is it not so evident to you that some people gain vitality, wisdom, charm, financial freedom, patience, have better sex, take better care of themselves, and have increasingly more fun as they age? They're out there. They're planning, learning, seeking, growing.

You should be one of them.

If, by the close of this book, we've helped you identify your goals and assemble a realistic and cohesive financial and life plan, we've earned our bells.

Most of all, we want you to enjoy a good, page-turning read. The Motley Fool's aim is ever to educate, to amuse, and to enrich. None without the other two. Onward, then, for an adventure, a laugh, and learning.

PART I

GET READY

Chapter One

Why Retire?

What is precious is never to forget
The delight of the blood drawn from ancient springs
Breaking through rocks in worlds before our earth;
Never to deny its pleasure in the simple morning light,
Nor its grave evening demand for love;
Never to allow gradually the traffic to smother
With noise and fog the flowering of the spirit.
—STEPHEN SPENDER

 YOU DON'T ACTUALLY want to retire, do you?
Why?
Just giving up? Or planning to walk away and play with your own toys?

Is it that you're trying to get somewhere or trying to escape where you've been?

You don't *actually* want to retire, do you?

Listen to what happened to our grandfathers.

A TALE OF TWO GRANDFATHERS

Our grandfathers were both accomplished and risk-loving entrepreneurs, one in Pennsylvania, the other in Washington, D.C.

Early last century, our Pennsylvania grandfather flew all around the North (occasionally the Great White North) selling saws. He sold his company, the modern-day DeWalt, to AMF in 1949. AMF eventually sold its DeWalt division to Black & Decker, where it remains a treasured brand. He retired at fifty-two. He loved investing and continued to do so successfully but never took another job in his life (he *did* treat the card game of bridge like a job, becoming a master before he died).

Our Washington, D.C., grandfather played football at Georgetown University, started his own insurance company after college, eventually bought a minority ownership in the Washington Senators baseball team (later the Minnesota Twins), and continued to go to the office every day until at the age of ninety, when his legs wouldn't take him anymore. He never intended to retire.

Did he need to go down to that office every day until the age of ninety? No.

And yes.

He probably did need to, because he loved to. He was a passionate man with a true Irish temper, and wanting was needing for him.

Both of these men made great impressions on us. But one of them made his impression over the first six years of our lives: Our early-retired Pennsylvania grandfather died relatively young, at the age of seventy-two. We cherish memories of his rascal's grin and propensity for secretly slipping us gumdrops minutes before supper was served. Sad to say, though, that's where the recollections end; we see him from afar, ever with the eyes of little boys.

By contrast, our Washington, D.C., grandfather charmed, influenced, and occasionally scared the dickens out of us for the first thirty-five years of our lives, leaving indelible marks until his eventual death in 2001 at the age of ninety-eight. One of those indelible marks was his lifelong lesson—born out of and borne out by his longevity—to stay active and engaged in the deeds of this world.

He who did not retire, never thinking to do so, died at ninety-eight.

God bless them both.

WHAT ARE YOU LIVING FOR?

We're certainly not here to suggest one family's recent history proves that working long equals living long. Leaving the working world does not automatically reduce one's life expectancy! That said, we tell the story because we do believe you increase your chances for extended happiness with *the approach you take to the future* when you're fifty-six or sixty-six—every bit as much as twenty-six or sixteen!

So we should reframe our thinking.

That's a necessity, given the regrettable but pervasive associations that the word "retirement" has in our society. Most people, of course, use it to refer to those days after the conclusion of formal full-time work: "Congratulations to Bob, who is retiring today following thirty-seven years of postal delivery"—or "To Susan, who is retiring after two decades of leading this august organization."

Do we really want to say this? Because here's the way it comes out: "*So long,* Susan," we think—bye-bye, Bob. "Retirement" carries heavy baggage, with its implications of departure and resignation. Standing there with a drink in your hand lifted for a retirement toast, it's hard not to think, "Their worthwhile days, their recorded life and times, are over." Do Susan and Bob want to be written off this way?

They probably don't think anything of it. Given the constant use of this word "retire"—which we'll avoid using ourselves as much as possible in this book—Bob and Susan are probably subconsciously falling into the same thinking, which is what happens when you're constantly exposed to a given word and its underlying concept without questioning its claims on you.

Listen, retirement is exactly what we should be trying to *avoid* in our lives, unless we're talking about the ultimate retirement. Up until that point, we should focus on the present and the future, asking what more we can learn, who else to help, how better to live day to day, all the questions that have always been asked and answered by human beings looking to improve their lots.

So let's please agree not to refer to any period of our lives as "retirement." We should almost always shoot for its exact opposite: *engagement.* Engagement will make you forget to ask yourself, "What are you retiring from?" Engagement asks the very much more relevant and interesting question: *"What are you living for?"*

This is a fine question for so many people to ask at (more) frequent intervals of their lives; your harried authors are again reminded of this even as we write and suggest it. The great thing about heading toward the second half of your life is that not only are you old enough to recognize the importance of asking "What am I living for?," but you're also young enough to fully exploit all of the opportunities wrapped up in the answers.

What are you living for?

If you've been traversing these past few decades asking yourself when you will retire, replace any fantasies of escape with something much better: the answers to that key question. Because another synonym for "retire" is "withdraw"—which provides the perfect play on words when we recognize that withdrawal is exactly the condition so often faced by those who leave the working world only to discover that disengaging from its society can be a hollow experience.

Why retire?

FOR FURTHER THINKING

Boxer George Foreman on why he came out of retirement:

Tom: After a ten-year retirement, you decided to fight again. You came back in 1987. Why did you come out of retirement?
George Foreman: For ten years I stood as an evangelist. I had this dynamic experience back in '77 after my last boxing match as *"The* George Foreman." I lost. I had a religious experience in the dressing room. I had a vision, and in a split second I was dead and alive again. On my hands and on my forehead, I started screaming because I saw blood. "Jesus Christ has come alive in me!" Of course, they rushed me to the emergency room. *(Laughter.)* But I will never forget that experience, to have a vision of death and life again. And I had a second chance to live. It changed me. For ten years I couldn't even shadowbox. But something happened. I got broke. I wish I had been a golfer, believe me. But because I was a boxer, that was my only profession, and I had to come back. Of course, the high point was to regain the title in 1994, [when I] defeated Michael Moore. It was unbelievable, because people tell you, look, you are a middle-aged man."
David: How old were you then, George?
Foreman: I was forty-five years old. The oldest man to ever become heavyweight champ of the world.
David: Have you ever thought about breaking that record?

Foreman: I do. I think about it all the time. I told my wife just the other day, "Look, David Toole was about to fight Lennox Lewis for the title. They couldn't agree on money." I said to my wife, "Look, I can pay David Toole that money he wants. If he is a number one contender, I can beat him. Then Lennox Lewis has got to fight me. I can be the heavyweight champion of the world." I went on for about two hours. After I finished, she said, "Shut up. Go lie down." *(Laughter.)* So when it gets to the point that you are more afraid of what your wife is going to do to you than Lennox Lewis and Mike Tyson, then it is time to leave it alone.

IT'S OKAY TO ASPIRE TO COUCHPOTATODOM, TOO

Okay, we hope we've at least challenged your thinking about retirement, and whether it's even desirable. We intentionally take a radical view to make as strong a case as we can for *not* retiring, since most of the treatment this topic gets assumes that retirement is the Ultimate Goal of All Your Working Years. While our argument may not be a mainstream one, it is bolstered by some mainstream numbers. An AARP study reported in *BusinessWeek* (October 2002) reveals that 69 percent of workers forty-five and over say they plan to work "in some capacity" during their golden years, including 34 percent—a full one out of three Americans— who said they would work part-time entirely *"for interest or enjoyment's sake"* (italics ours).

We also hasten to add that some people truly wish to stop taking any salary of any kind and just rest, relax, relax some more, rest again, etc. Occasionally, when we're wearied by work, this sounds really good to us, too. We don't mean to suggest that dedicating one's latter days to relaxation for its own sake is bad or wrong. We do mean to challenge you to look deeper when we ask the questions "Why retire?" and "What are you living for?"

FINANCIAL INDEPENDENCE,
NOT RETIREMENT

One simple and delightful term that we have had frequent occasion to use in past Motley Fool writings, both online and off-, is "financial independence." This is what so many of us are shooting for with our work and financial efforts. For those efforts, financial independence is a worthy end. Yet—and here's the crux—*it is not just an end but also primarily a means.*

Financial independence, wonderful achievement that it is, is most of all a means that enables you to live a life of opportunity and choice—in a word, one of our very favorite words, FREEDOM. It is this freedom that we yearn most deeply for, for ourselves and our children. It isn't about being rich, and indeed there isn't any single amount that objectively makes Americans rich, or officially earns them financial independence. It's all relative. It's about being able to do what *you* want to in life, what would give *you* the most gratification and joy—we all define these things differently—untrammeled by worries or concerns over money. "Mere money," we should say.

To us, financial independence is a concept virtually synonymous with the American Dream. It's what America was designed to achieve for its citizens. No surprise that it continues to happen to more people here than in many other countries of this world *combined.*

Are you living the American Dream? Not yet? Well, if not, it's our aim to help get you there. If you're forty or over and find that you lack knowledge in one or more key areas of your finances, peruse again our table of contents and notice that each chapter has a relevant topic for anyone forty and over who'll most likely confront a decision about that. This book is for people who want to make better financial decisions.

Are you living your American Dream?

Our American Dream isn't retirement!

Nor should it be yours.

"Why retire?" we ask. We think it a perfect way for Fools to begin a book ostensibly about retirement. No, no . . . the American Dream is *financial independence.* Being free to live where you want, how you want, and do what you want. Let's work to make that happen.

Action Plan

■ Prepare yourself to spend some time thinking through your future plans. It's not most people's favorite thing to do, but it's critical. Grab a notebook and dedicate it to your retirement planning. As you move through this book, you can jot down lists and thoughts and things to do.

■ Now ask yourself if you really want to retire. *Really,* we mean it. Take a minute and think it through. If you do want to retire, ask yourself why. Next, think about what you're living for and what engages you on this earth. What communities, big and small, are you in? Write down your thoughts and answers to these questions.

■ Make a list of people you admire who are in or near retirement—those whose lifestyles and degree of contentment impress you. Then identify exactly what it is you admire. Is it how efficiently Thelma gardens? Is it how Fred manages to be involved in a dozen different hobbies? Is it how Louise has done so much good in her community and always has a smile? Is it how George Foreman loves life? Figure out how they do what they do. Have a short talk with these folks, if possible. See how they budget their time and what their priorities are. Then think about how you can be like them, and what steps you'll need to take. In many cases, with a little effort, you can become the kind of person you admire most. That's a great way to live the rest of your life.

Chapter Two

Plan for Excellence

Whatever failures I have known, whatever errors I have committed,
whatever follies I have witnessed in private and public life have been
the consequence of action without thought.

—BERNARD BARUCH

 DEAR READER, we've played a trick on you, an innocent little trick.

We know that many book readers simply skip the dedication, the foreword, and the introduction to get right to the heart of the matter. And so we have covertly redirected our preparatory thoughts on How Best to Read This Book right here into our short and simple Chapter Two. We've spent years now studying and writing up our thoughts on financial independence for midlifers, which makes it that much more important to us that you effectively use this text.

For starters, you are *not* turning the pages of an airy how-to guide for influencing your friends, speculating in real estate, finding your inner child, then living free-spiritedly in retirement. Instead, in these pages, we'll be working together through the realities of financial stewardship. Some of them are tough realities. A few of you will learn that you have more work to do if you're to walk away from your job at age sixty-two. Others of you will blanch at the thought of having to design a first-rate will or determine the exact amount of health insurance you'll need today and for your future.

But our aims are clear. We don't want you to carry financial burdens, doubts, or anxieties into the second half of your life. Consequently, some of our chapters will read more like a critical *to-do* list than an inspirational *how-to* journey. That's how we believe we can serve you best. Other scholars far more versed in total wellness—for example, Dr. Mark Hyman in his book *Ultraprevention*—can give you the inside skinny on feeling better, living longer, and gaining energy as you age. The promise that *we* make to you is to give you the numbers and the actions you'll need to take to have more than enough money right up until the end of your glorious life.

This is a *to-do* book, not a *how-to* book.

Given that, we strongly recommend that you take each chapter and its assigned tasks at a comfortable pace. The most effective way to use this book is to read a chapter, complete all of the assignments, then take a few days off to celebrate your success. Catch a great movie, or crack open a 1992 bottle of Château Margaux Bordeaux, or head up into the mountains for a hike. Once there, pat yourself on the back with a "Daggum, now I've got all the health-care coverage I need!" Or a "How about that, I've optimized the college funds for my kids!" Celebrate your successes here, one chapter at a time.

Then, once refreshed, get back to work on the next chapter.

Our Motley Fool Travel Advisory (MFTA): Attempts to read this book straight through may well have the opposite effect than that which we intend. Our goal is to offer an elegant, simple yet sophisticated design for your retirement plans. Our goal is to get you on top of your finances, directing your affairs with all the efficiency and confidence of a veteran captain steering his mighty ship across the Aegean. But you simply can't get there *tomorrow*. You can't complete all that you'll need to by the middle of next week. If you try to tackle it all immediately, you're bound to conclude that managing your finances into and through retirement is simply impossible. And that might cause you to leave important tasks undone, or worse, to blindly delegate them into the hands of unscrupulous or incompetent advisors. That's a terrible downside for simply trying to do too much too fast while reading this book.

Heed our warning and, instead, complete the chapters and the tasks gradually, one by one. Set your goal. Make the plan. Get it done. Then take a day, or even a week off between chapters. When you're fresh and ready to return, dive back in with vim and vigor. The result will be a firm financial foundation for the rest of your life. You'll have your kids taken care of through college, your parents comfortable in their senior years, your debts repaid, your income saved, your assets organized, and all the financial support needed to fuel an excellent life from here.

Plan for excellence. Then pace yourself as you get done what you'll need to in order to live without financial concerns.

Let us begin.

FOR FURTHER THINKING

Whether building a financial plan or running a start-up, prepare for volatility. Here's Jeff Bezos, founder of Amazon.com, on the dot-com roller-coaster ride:

Tom: Over the course of the last three years in particular, it's been a roller-coaster ride for so many businesses. Jeff, did you ever imagine doing anything different?

Jeff Bezos: No. I am a change junkie. I love what we are doing. This is incredible fun. I guarantee you, this is still the very, very beginning. It may not be Kitty Hawk anymore, but nobody has even thought of the DC-9, much less the jet engine. There is a lot of innovation that is going to happen. This is such an incredibly fun place to be.

Action Plan

■ Take a few minutes to define your dreams and ambitions. Sketch out a time line for how and when you might achieve some or all of them. Many people don't spend enough time dreaming, while others do but never dare to achieve those dreams. With a little planning and discipline—with a time line—you might happily surprise yourself. Don't put this stuff off forever, or it will never get done.

■ As well as you can, determine the approximate cost of each dream and ambition. If you want to travel along the Nile one day, that will involve airfare, lodging, and meals, plus pretrip research (much of which you might do for free at your local library). If you've always wanted to learn to play the piano, call around and find out how much lessons will cost you.

■ Next, plan how you might achieve some—or all!—of your dreams. If you long to speak Portuguese, then see when in your schedule you can make time for classes. If you enjoy sailing and want to buy a boat, then figure out how you might be able to save for a vessel.

■ A final useful exercise to help you think about what you want to achieve in life is thinking about what your legacy will be, what you'll leave behind. If you have children, you've already created a legacy that will survive you. But children aside, perhaps you'd like to donate enough money to buy a piece of art for a place you love, or to write a book or create an endowment fund for your favorite charity. Give this subject some thought.

PART II

HAVING ENOUGH

Chapter Three

What Is Enough, and for How Long?

Enough is equal to a feast.
—HENRY FIELDING

 THE POSSIBILITIES FOR life after leaving the nine-to-five workforce are endless. These possibilities are truly circumscribed only by your imagination.

Right?

Er, wait . . . you say not so?

You say that's an incredibly naive statement typical of the sort of self-help books that you specifically brushed *past* in order to purchase this more practical (you thought) book?

All right, you win. Just remember that sarcasm is the wit of Fools. Because the possibilities for life after regular employment are in fact limited by a host of different factors:

There's that mortgage you still have to pay.

The utility bills, too.

Don't forget about the dental and podiatrist visits.

Plus, the dog still needs heartworm pills—the good kind. And the lawn guy won't magically start trimming the bougainvilleas out of the kindness of his heart.

Put any amount of thought into what you'll be doing during retirement, and you may even face a few *new* line items in your budget—how about increased travel expenses, craft-club dues (hey, we're just thinking out loud here), maybe even the cost of training for a new career.

Independence is still so very dependent. Even when you're completely financially independent—laudable achievement and state that it is—your choices are limited by factors from how much money you have to your general level of energy, number of dependents, and willingness to try new things.

In this chapter we're going to focus on the "how much money you have" part. The foundation of good financial planning for your later years is *knowing if you'll be able to cover your expenses,* year in and year out. From the words of an elder member who is financially independent and posts on our discussion boards at Fool.com: "One of the biggest problems with retirement planning is deciding how much you spend every year. I'm surviving because I've done my homework."

Let's do a little homework!

THE COSTS OF RETIREMENT

Despite the rumors, retirement is not some long-awaited lottery payout. Sure, you may have scrimped and saved over the years to build a fortune that's in the six digits or higher. But that money has to carry you through many decades (knock on wood) of living and playing expenses.

Pundits say that you'll need 60 to 80 percent of your present gross income to live comfortably in retirement. Unfortunately, that assumption is outdated. Those calculations assume you'll receive a comfortable pension from your lifelong employer, that you won't develop many new interests, and that you'll most likely live to the ripe old age of seventy-two. As most of us know, we tend to have several employers—if not a dozen—during our lifetime. With all the new soy products available, we're living longer lives than any previous generation (is soy really that good for you? we ask). Seriously, baby boomers are healthier than any American generation heading into the second half of life. With our health intact, we might as well pick up a few new, and usually not free, hobbies.

Most people blow the 60-to-80-percent rule out of the water

(ka-BOOM!) during the first five or so years of retirement. When they finally retire, it's like spring break in Fort Lauderdale for the older crowd—they go nuts on golf courses, in boats, along seashores. They do all those things they were previously able to during only seventeen vacation days a year.

"Check, please!"

They forget that the last five or so years of life can also be budget busters, since medical costs tend to eat into savings. That's especially true if you have a drawn-out illness or need twenty-four-hour care. Talk about sticker shock.

Still, when it comes to having enough money to live on during retirement—just enough—the 60-to-80-percent rule is at least a start. So that's where we'll begin: with the bare necessities.

TODAY'S BUDGET

To begin to calculate the amount needed to maintain your current standard of living, let's take the logical route and calculate the cost of—you guessed it—your present standard of living. If you're not the type of person who giddily keeps a color-coded, multitabulated budget, then here's a quick-and-dirty way to figure it out:

(1) Gather a month's worth of paychecks. Voila! There's the income side of your ledger.

(2) Now add up the must-pay bills—you know, the stuff that keeps you fed with a roof over your head and a comfortable indoor temperature of 71.3 degrees. These must-pay bills include: your mortgage or rent, utilities, insurance payments (take the annual cost and divide it by twelve), groceries, your current retirement contributions, etc.

(3) Subtract your must-pay bills from your income, and you have a cursory take on your current discretionary income, or the money you have left over.

This represents a really, really rough estimate of your current cash flow. The more specific you can be in assessing current expenses, the fewer surprises will rear their ugly head in the future. (If you want to get into the nitty-gritty of building a full-blown budget, consider using a program like Quicken and picking up *The Motley Fool Personal Finance Workbook*.)

TOMORROW'S EXPENSES

If you don't envision a dramatic lifestyle change in retirement, then estimating your future expenses is straightforward. The three biggest costs for later life are:

(1) **Your home.** Despite what some might have you believe, the majority of Americans don't immediately move into a tidy little Senior Hacienda upon conclusion of their formal employment. Why leave all your friends when you have more time to enjoy them? Shelter continues to be a big cost. We offer strategies for deftly handling this big expense in Chapter 8, "Owning the Right Home."

(2) **Your extracurricular activities.** What is the second half of your life if not open season for extracurricular activities? As with the ice-skating and cello lessons from your childhood, most adult activities carry a price tag. To be prepared, start getting estimates. For example: To golfers, that means projecting costs for the course fees, the lessons, the club replacements (from general wear and tear, please, not a fit on the eighteenth tee!), etc.

(3) **Your health.** When you're figuring out how much retirement will cost, you need to take a magnifying glass to your insurance coverage. This is one expense that can seem to increase exponentially as you age. Funding your health and medical costs is the main topic of Chapter 9.

Costs You Won't Incur in Later Life

Now for the good news! Some of the costs of being will disappear once you transform into Your New and Improved Self. Here are some:

- Social Security taxes (if you're not working at all)
- Job-related expenses, such as dry cleaning and commuting
- Retirement-plan contributions

- Child-related costs (unless you had children much later in life)
- Education and professional-development costs
- Disability and life-insurance premiums
- The mortgage (depending on how long you've owned your home)
- The office birthday collection

TODAY'S INVESTMENTS

Next, let's see what your future employer is going to pay you. Your future "salary" comes from five major sources of income:

(1) Social Security: We cover this thoroughly in Chapter 10, but you can get an estimate of your future benefits at www.ssa.gov.
(2) Employer-provided pensions: Get an estimate from your plan provider.
(3) Personal savings (taxable accounts, 401(k)/403(b)/457 plans, IRAs, Keoghs, etc.): Add up the current market value of all of these investments, including your regular savings account.
(4) Work (if you continue to earn a wage)
(5) Other (inheritances, home equity, collections, etc.)

OKAY, SO HOW MUCH WILL YOU NEED?

With a grasp of your current and future expenses, as well as a rough idea of how much you've already saved to pay your future self, you can estimate whether you have enough to retire . . .

. . . except there are a few niggling details to ponder first. To wit, for how many years will you draw on those sources of income? What will inflation be over that period? And will you be cashing out your starting retirement portfolio to support your income needs, or aiming to live off the earnings while never touching the principal? And what about your taxes?

If you can answer just those questions, you can determine what you'll need to support you for the rest of your life. But if you're like most people, that litany of questions occasions an altogether unpleasant queasiness.

Don't abandon ship yet.

For now let's forget about the details. We won't even consider inflation. We'll ignore Social Security, too, and disregard any company pension you may get. Let's pretend your money gets no return now or after retirement. We'll count only what you've saved for retirement as of today.

Let's say that amounts to $20,000.

Further, let's say you want an annual income of $30,000 in today's dollars after you finish work, that you will retire in twenty-five years, that you will live twenty years after that, and that you expect to meet your maker waving your last dollar bill.

Reread that last sentence to grasp our assumptions cleanly.

Okay, so how much do you need to amass by the start of your retirement, and how much do you have to save each year between now and then to get there?

Let's see. First things first, $30,000 a year for 20 years comes to $600,000 needed for an independent retirement. You already have $20,000 of that, so you're $580,000 short. Divide the shortage by the 25 years you have to save it up, and you need to generate savings of $23,200 *annually* between now and the time you stop drawing income.

That was oversimple, but on purpose, just to show you that the hard part isn't figuring this stuff out or planning for it. For the scenario above, the hard part is five figures' worth of annual savings. We'll have lots more advice for you about obtaining additional savings and investing them better, most notably in Chapters 5 and 6.

FOR FURTHER THINKING

Keep your expectations under control, and you can't help but succeed. Here's Loretta Lynn on money and happiness:

David: Loretta, some people say money ensures happiness. Do you?

Loretta Lynn: No. It doesn't. I think if you got a good bed to crawl into when you are sleepy and you have a good warm meal . . . that is about as good as you can get it. I wouldn't ask for more.

HOW LONG WILL IT LAST?

Shifting into a higher gear of understanding takes more math and a dash more technology. We've already sneaked into the mathematics of retirement planning (shhhhhh!), but if you're serious about this topic and your financial plans, you should put away the legal pad and click in to one of several available financial-software tools, like Quicken Financial Planner or one of our retirement calculators at Fool.com. Quicken Financial Planner costs money, whereas our retirement calculators are free, but in either case your retirement plans are certainly worth at least the effort, if not the money.

If you're gagging at the thought of going through with this, please note that other help exists: A financial planner can help you think through what's below, particularly if you don't feel sufficiently motivated or equipped to do it. (You may wish to flip to Chapter 7 right now, where we'll show you how to find a *good* financial pro who is working *for* you—which shouldn't ever be assumed.)

Okay, time to input the data. You will begin to see via the calculators how *inflation, taxes, investment returns,* and *your life expectancy* all affect your plans. You'll typically be asked to provide numbers other than just the expenses and income we've already considered. These include:

Your expected "withdrawal rate." The goal for most retirees may be fairly summed up this way: "Each year I'll chip away as much as I can at my nest egg without ever shattering it." The term "withdrawal rate" describes in percentage terms how much you can take from your savings and still be reasonably sure you'll have enough left over to meet your long-term needs.

There have been lots of studies on withdrawal rates. One of the best was compiled by three Trinity University professors—Philip Cooley, Carl Hubbard, and Daniel Walz—who examined historical annual returns for stocks and bonds from 1926 through 1995. The study revealed that over periods longer than fifteen years, withdrawal rates exceeding 5 percent severely threaten the shell of the nest egg.

The authors reached five very useful conclusions that you can test out as you tinker with a calculator:

(1) Younger retirees who anticipate longer payout periods should plan on lower withdrawal rates.

(2) Bonds increase the success rate for lower to midlevel withdrawal rates, but most retirees would benefit with at least a 50 percent allocation to stocks.

(3) Retirees who hope to withdraw more dollars to match inflation must accept a substantially reduced withdrawal rate from the initial portfolio.

(4) Stock-dominated portfolios using a 3 to 4 percent withdrawal rate may create rich heirs at the expense of the retiree's current consumption.

(5) For fifteen-year-or-less payout periods, a withdrawal rate of 8 to 9 percent from a stock-dominated portfolio has worked— though after the bear market we've just lived through, we doubt that scenario looks as rosy these days.

We will be covering withdrawal rates in more detail later, including updated numbers for the optimal withdrawal rate in Chapter 15, "So You're Retired Already, Eh?"

The future rate of inflation. Consider a $1,000 monthly income that fails to increase with the cost of living (assuming inflation runs 4 percent annually). That $1,000 will buy only $555 worth of today's goods in fifteen years. To protect your purchasing power in the future, you must save enough today to increase your income in retirement. Either that or cut back to 55.5 percent of the caviar and champagne you're tossing back nightly. Four percent is a conservative estimate, meaning that inflation over the next couple of decades should average lower. Why? Because last century our Treasury and Federal Reserve figured out that the growth in money supply is the single greatest creator of inflation, so we can expect our future monetary policy to be smarter. Anyway, 4 percent is probably high, but we prefer to be conservative when making such estimates. That way, surprises tend to be pleasant.

Your expected returns from investments. No one can predict what you'll earn on your money; that's why we've always tended to consult history. And history tells us (via the research of Ibbotson Associates) that for the years 1926 through 2000, the average annual total return of the S&P 500 was 11.1 percent; the annual average total return for long-term corporate bonds was 5.7 percent; and inflation averaged 3.1 percent per year. That means a portfolio constructed of a 75 percent holding in the S&P 500 and a 25 percent holding of long-term corporate bonds would have produced an average annual return of about 9.75 percent. A few more comparisons: A 60 percent stock/40 percent bond portfolio would have posted an annual average return of 8.9 percent, while the average annual return on a 50/50 portfolio would have been about 8.4 percent. When projecting your investment returns, start by using the above average annual numbers. Here again you can make your surprises pleasant ones by being conservative.

Your life expectancy. Hey, even if it's a bit creepy, considering the time of your demise is a necessary part of retirement planning. If you want to make sure you don't outlive your money, you have to have an idea how long you're going to live. For the purposes of retirement planning, you can get as specific or general as you want. You can also track some pretty sophisticated and interesting longevity tests by searching "longevity test" at www.google.com. For now let's forgo the full-body MRI and simply consider how long some of your blood relatives lived. The average American life span is about seventy-seven years. As you might expect, playing it safe here means tacking on another ten years or so to your life expectancy, for the purpose of your calculations. You should be so lucky!

Amount in taxes you'll pay in retirement. Taxes in retirement can be complicated. Some part of your Social Security benefit will definitely not be taxable, but some may be. Distributions from a traditional IRA count as ordinary income, but distributions from a Roth IRA do not. With every check you receive from your annuity provider, one portion is taxable and one portion is a return of your original investment. We'd like to say there's an easy way to estimate what your taxes will be in retirement. Unfortunately, we can't.

If you have access to a tax-software program, such as Turbo Tax, then running a simulation is your best bet. The Internal Revenue Service website provides a list of companies that provide online tax-preparation services. Many will allow you to do a simulation for free, charging only when you file your taxes or print your return. Knowing your precise tax rate in retirement is not absolutely crucial; however, the amount you pay in taxes will affect what you have left over for room and shuffleboard, so it's an exercise worth completing in the not-too-distant future.

Armed with this data, you can determine the annual savings required to enjoy the good life. We can't end this chapter as ingenious *Hitchhiker's Guide to the Galaxy* author Douglas Adams might have, by saying, "It's 42!" That's because the "it" in this case is all relative. We all have different income amounts coming from different sources, and varying expectations (and realities) about how much we'll spend in our postwork years. What we've tried to do in this chapter is provide you a framework that you can use to plug in your own numbers, then plan with confidence how much money you'll need to achieve financial independence for a period of a decade or more.

An advantage to working some of this out on your own—the true Foolish spirit of learning from others to do for yourself—is that you are able to play "what if" games. With the help of a financial calculator, tool, or advisor, you can quickly vary your scenarios by tweaking things like inflation, rates of return, date of retirement, and desired income levels. Please do play these what-if games. They'll convey to you a much deeper sense of the variety of outcomes than if you just look at one scenario and treat it as the rigid and inevitable "truth." So again: Massage the calculator. Play with, nurture, and love the calculator. It will impose an excellent combination of open-mindedness and resolve upon those who take the time to ask, "Okay, yeah . . . but what if?"

There you have our introduction to "What is enough, and for how long?": the financial operating instructions for figuring out your later years. Ahead we'll tackle elements of your plan, as well as a host of other considerations.

Action Plan

■ Gather your important papers. A handful of financial records will provide most of the data you'll need to figure out your dream retirement. Don't worry—you don't need every receipt for every expense from the past forty years. Just try to find the most recent of the following:

❑ Checking-account statement(s)
❑ Credit-card bill(s)
❑ IRA and/or 401(k) (or 403(b), SEP, etc.) statements
❑ Mortgage statements
❑ Brokerage records
❑ Social Security statement (you can request one at www.ssa.gov)
❑ Savings account/CD/money-market account records
❑ Secret Bahamian account statements written with invisible ink

■ From the data you gathered above, draft a very rough budget. Account for your cash inflows and outflows and list your investments. This will help you see how much you have and how much money is coming into and going out of your bank account.

■ Tinker with some retirement calculators. There are several ways to figure out how much income will come in during your golden years. There's one method we Fools particularly like—we think you know this by now—using a calculator! We're fond of Quicken's package or the retirement calculator we use on our site. (To find that, head to Fool.com and search for "retirement" or "calculators.")

■ To quote *The Hitchhiker's Guide to the Galaxy* a second time: "Don't Panic." Does the retirement calculator say you need to save an additional $10,000 per month and also work a decade after your death? Eeeesh. Well, buck up and keep flipping pages—more help ahead. Plus, constantly remind yourself that even if you can't create the perfect scenario, *every step you take in a positive direction* does directly improve your fortunes.

Chapter Four

Helping Yourself First

Nothing strengthens the judgment and quickens the conscience like individual responsibility.

—Elizabeth Cady Stanton

 WHEN WE FIRST proposed this chapter title, our baby-boomer friend Phil Marti would have none of it. "I hate to tell you this," he said, "but you're pushing just about my biggest button. The *last* thing my generation needs to be reminded of is putting oneself first. We're the most self-absorbed, self-gratifying generation in history."

We'll let you, dear reader, agree or disagree with Phil's contention on your own. For our part, we think it comes down to what is actually *meant* by "help yourself first."

Is this "help yourself" as in dash over to the buffet, knock back the elderly gentleman in the green suit, and load up on the dumplings before anyone else gets a shot? "Help yourself" to the choicest cut of meat? Chisel your initials into the biggest slice of pie? Assuredly not. Indeed, quite unFoolish (remember, "Foolish" to us means handsomely fighting against bad conventional wisdom—"unFoolish" is a nasty term in this book).

No, Phil and other critics of your generation, we mean "help" more in the sense of "Take care of yourself, lest you be unable to take care of others." There's surely some selfishness in there, but if you object to that, appreciate the invisible hand of its attendant altruism.

Because he is best prepared to help others who has already helped himself.

Sound familiar? Put another way elsewhere: "The Lord helps those who help themselves." Here it is in modern-day speech, courtesy of L.A. attorney and Motley Fool member Bob Shore: "In airplanes, the concept is 'Rescuers first.' In the event of sudden cabin depressurization, the adult should put his or her own oxygen mask on first, and only then assist any children or elderly with their oxygen masks. The reason isn't selfishness, it's practical. If you don't take care of yourself, you can't take care of others."

We're framing this chapter mainly as "you versus the younger generations." We certainly believe you should be helping your parents to the best of your abilities, and we've devoted a chapter (Chapter 11) to that topic. But getting back to the younger generations, there are at least two excellent reasons we're promoting "rescuers first" right here, right now.

WHO HAS THE (EARNINGS) POWER?

First, consider the relative positions of you versus, say, your hypothetical teenager. Your teenager has fifty or more years of income-earning power; you have ten to twenty. In a pinch, your teenager can borrow cheaply to fund his or her education. Student loans typically carry interest rates that are about half what you'd pay on a credit card.

This is all to say that an extra dollar is better put toward your own later years than your child's schooling. Students can work their way through school when necessary. More important, they can earn partial or full college scholarships or receive many different forms of financial aid. (We'll be covering this more in Chapter 12, "Paying for Your Kids and College.") Where are the scholarships for adults?

The point is quite simple, though perhaps it sounds contrary: *Don't* worry so much about funding your kids' college education that you neglect your own old-age financial planning. Help yourself first. Our children are in a much more financially advantageous position, primarily as a function of their age, than we their parents, many earnings years removed. It'll be a lot easier for a young woman to scrape for her education in her late teens or early twenties than for her mother to salvage her own broken finances at age sixty-four.

Financial planning for your sunset decades, and the accompanying success, comes *first*.

ROLE MODEL

A second excellent reason for "rescuers first" is that those who practice it successfully serve as influential role models for family and friends.

We have our parents to thank or to blame for so many things, our conceptions about money among them. How Mom and Dad handled their money powerfully affects our approach to the green stuff, even in ways we tend to forget, since these are so deeply ingrained in us. And we're not just talking about paying off debt or investing in stocks.

In our case, we were raised by a father who emphasized spending money on experiences rather than objects. Dad has always said that experiences provide more gratification both in the present and in lasting memories and bonds of love and friendship—in contrast to purchasing, well, things. That, too, is an approach to money, yet one that has implications whose fingers reach deep into our psyche.

Please know that how you are handling your money today, as a "grown-up," and in the years to come is gradually and invisibly (but oh so tellingly) laying one little foundation stone after another—the foundation of your children's approach to money when *they* are grown-ups. Is Mom or Dad going to borrow recklessly, then play the victim as the interest charges come due? Or is Mom or Dad going to be organized and disciplined in day-to-day spending?

These things rub off and come back to help or to haunt you years later, when you need a little help from your children. Which is why the strong effort toward—or even better, successful demonstration of—true self-sufficiency in your finances is so potent. Helping yourself first will help your kids even in ways you may not be counting on.

As a relevant side note, we should mention that we recently published the bestselling *Motley Fool Investment Guide for Teens,* which can help provide the young people in your life with a good grounding in saving and investing; both will benefit them in the future if they get a good understanding now.

THE RIGHT WAY TO THINK ABOUT THIS

The ideal is to be able to fund both yourself and your extended family. If, after maxing out your matched 401(k) and IRA deductions, you still have good money left over, *wunderbar.* Invest heavily in your children!

If you are one of the many boomers who find themselves toeing the financial line, recognize that your own lack of financial security may wind up a greater burden to your children than their burden of not having had the best and most expensive education (and life) possible.

But let's not, as we did above, dwell in extremes. Middle ground exists aplenty. A particularly good example comes from those who started a family relatively early and have years to earn even after their children have graduated. Motley Fool member Wilauc (screen name) is a very fine example:

> For the past 17 years our biggest annual expense has been school tuition for our kids. I probably should mention that we've been living in Tokyo since 1985, and elected to send our two sons to a private "international" school. That works out to 25 years of tuition fees (1–12 for one child, K–12 for the other), well in excess of $300,000. Add to that college tuition–both boys elected to go to a top liberal arts college in the U.S., and we were happy to support them in their choice. So by the time the younger of our sons graduates in another two years, the total we've spent on education will be approaching a half million dollars. And that doesn't count what we've paid over the years for music lessons, extra language lessons, et cetera. Being educated is about more than just "book learning"!

Bottom line: We're very happy with the education our kids have received, and consider the money well spent. Sure, it would be great to have that half million sitting in a retirement account, to be used someday for a life of leisure (assuming we live that long). But we don't regret the choice we made and would do it all again. OK, so that means I don't own a home (renting) and have less than $100K saved for retirement—and no pension (though my wife will have one) and minimal Social Security. On the other hand, I have another 15 years to go until I reach retirement age (and really don't plan to fully "retire" from working then). Now that our "investment" is starting to pay off (elder son is gainfully employed), the $25K per year that had been going toward tuition can start going toward retirement.

He closed by asking rhetorically, "Where's the joy in having a comfortable retirement fund if your kids are struggling to make ends meet on a minimum-wage job because they don't have the education and skills to get anything better?"

In a chapter entitled "Help Yourself First," that excerpt may seem out of place. But it's quite well placed, because we're not here to suggest "the only way is to protect yourself," nor are we interested in providing one simplistic viewpoint. Our primary aim has been to challenge the thinking of many who might nod silently and acquiescingly at Wilauc's statement—and then wind up creating even greater and undue burdens on themselves and their children-turned-adults years later. The challenge, as we see it, is to set the example of self-reliance or self-provision. When you choose to make sacrifices for your children, explain to them the reasons and results of that decision. While we favor securing yourself in retirement before spending excessively on the education of your children, we can accept the contrary—so long as your children know where the money came from, learn self-reliance from you, and buy you that mansion in the suburbs with their Nobel Prize money.

All of these aims can be served, a perfect balance struck, for any of us who perfects better spending habits. We doubt we're shocking you or impressing you with that. But we're going to go one better by providing, in the next chapter, numerous tips that anyone can use to save substantially more.

Action Plan

■ Outline the goals and demands putting pressure on your retirement saving and investing. For example, are you having trouble saving for retirement because you're also saving or paying for your kid's college education? Become aware of what is standing in the way of (or just hampering, to some degree) building your all-important retirement nest egg.

■ Spend some time thinking about how to reconcile the demands above with your need to save for your golden years. Jot down and then explore some alternative plans. For example, if you're struggling to save for Junior's college education, look into less expensive schools and/or scholarships, or jump ahead to Chapter 12 to discover college savings options now. (Not all scholarships are for the smartest or most athletic kid—many are for average kids who are interested in certain subjects or hail from certain regions or have certain other traits.) If you've been saving to travel around the world, look into less expensive ways to do so. (If you can afford to save for retirement *and* meet your other goals, peachy; ignore this action item.)

■ Get your children thinking about money management and involve them in the family finances. Even when they're fairly young, you can begin teaching them about saving and smart spending. We offer more specific suggestions in Chapter 13. But for starters, give them allowances and/or let them earn some money from you. As they get older, start them in some modest stock investments, and encourage them to get part-time jobs. With planning and discipline, your kids can take some of the burden of paying for college off your shoulders by contributing savings of their own. Teens and preteens can gain some painless and profitable insights into the financial world via our book *The Motley Fool Investment Guide for Teens: 8 Steps to Having More Money Than Your Parents Ever Dreamed Of*. They can also click over to www.Fool.com/teens.

Chapter Five

The Game of Increased Savings

Use it up, wear it out, make it do, or do without.
—Traditional New England adage

 We love games of all sorts.

Our childhood was spent sneaking hours long past our bedtime, stretching out school nights past one A.M. to play board games lit by flashlight—to the consternation of our parents. Cross-legged on our bedroom floor, we rolled dice on felt, flipped cards hushedly, slid counters from square to square, and kept score like greedy bankers. We have continued to treat life as a strategy game— serious fun that appeals to the intellect, which is, like all good games, occasionally unpredictable.

Your personal finances can be played like a game as well: serious fun that appeals to the intellect and is, like all good games, occasionally unpredictable. Had we all been taught to play "money as a limited resource in the quest for economic freedom," how much useless junk would we *not* have bought along the way? How many dollars would we have set aside in 401(k) and IRA plans? How thoroughly would we have involved our entire family in the savings game? And frankly, how much more fun would we have had along the way?

Never mind the past now. The future still provides ample opportunity to move the Terrier or Laundry Iron or Top Hat of our finances around the Monopoly board of savings.

As you may have surmised, this chapter aims to help you find as many ways as possible to save more money. To stay true to our character, we present these in the form of eight different games. They are offered from easiest and most enjoyable (getting organized) to most challenging (signing up for a second job).

Let's commence!

#1. THE "ONE-MONTH MYSTERY" GAME

The first bit of enterprise is one for us all, no matter our means. Set a shoe box on the floor of your office or den (in between the pile of unopened mail and the dusty NordicTrack). Over the next calendar month, pitch all your receipts into that box. Grocery bills, mortgage payment, cable bill, restaurant and coffee receipts, utilities, clothing, the cost of that blender from Williams-Sonoma, the airplane ticket to Denver, plants from the nursery, any bill and every bill. Take all the receipts and drop them into the shoe box.

At the end of the month, spend two hours separating your receipts into two groups:

Group 1: Necessity

Group 2: Luxury

We set those off on the page to make it plain where we're headed in the One-Month Mystery. Let's break them out.

You needed the yogurt and the shampoo; you needed to make the mortgage and utility payments; and you needed to pay for your daughter's eyeglasses. Those go in the **Necessity** pile. But did you need to buy another business suit? Did you need three new music CDs? Did you need full treatment at the spa and that dinner at Bistrot Lepic Wine Bar? Probably not. Place them in the **Luxury** stack.

Some items will be difficult to classify. Is cable television a need or want? The furniture reupholstery, the high-speed Internet access, tickets to the opera—needs or wants? Do your best to distinguish each. For a professional photographer, the new camera equipment was likely a need. For the rest of us, score the tripod and wide-angle lens as luxuries.

You now have a full month of expenses broken into two categories.

Next, simply multiply the combined total by twelve. This is a ballpark estimate of your annual expenses. It isn't perfect, because some expenses are sporadic and didn't show up in the one month you tracked. But you do have a ballpark figure. With that number in hand, you qualify as a candidate for chief financial officer at WorldCom. (Talk about an upgrade for WorldCom.)

Now it's time to ask what you've learned from all this filing and counting.

Start by comparing your total annual expenses to your total annual income after taxes. Divide total annual expenses by total annual take-home income to see, in percentage terms, how much of your take-home pay you're spending each year. You should be saving anywhere from 10 to 20 percent of your take-home pay.

Next, stack up your necessity expenses against the costs for things you merely wanted. Are you spending more on needs or wants? And by how much? If you're like most Americans, it's time to look very carefully at what you're really getting for all those luxuries in life.

You've solved the one-month mystery of your spending. Which leads us to game number two . . .

FOR FURTHER THINKING

Saving money is as much about perspective as anything. Here's the late Fred Rogers (Mister Rogers) on growing up during the depression:

Fred Rogers: I think most of us who grew up in the Depression are quite conscious of being careful with money and other things. I recycle everything I possibly can find. I'll stop my car and pick up a plastic bottle on the street and take it home to recycle. When the tenor of the whole country is such that every thing is limited, that sticks with you. I was only two, three, four years old at that time. Yet you get those attitudes from the people that you live with, those who are closest to you.

#2. THE "SPARTAN LIFE" GAME

Let us explore the simple math of longevity. If you live to the grand old age of ninety, you'll have spent 1,080 months on this earth. If you're fifty today and you live to ninety, that leaves you 480 months of oxygen. Would it not be prudent to dedicate one of those months to the game of pure necessity?

We hear you shouting across the nation, "Yes, but how?"

Okay, maybe not shouting. But curious?

All right. So you're not curious. We'll shoot for *willing*. Are you willing to live lean for thirty days just to get a read on the real necessity costs of your life?

Ah, yes. Good.

Here's how.

It's time to live a Spartan's life for just four weeks. Instead of going on a shopping spree, put yourself on a temporary spending freeze.

Simply file away the receipts, classification, and calculation of all the luxuries from the One-Month Mystery game. You won't be spending that money this month. You are left with the receipts, categories, and calculations of the basic necessities of your life. Guess what? That represents your budget for the next four weeks. Allocate just that amount of money and prepare yourself to enjoy the little things in life—warm soup, a neighborhood jog, your daughter's soccer game, an excellent documentary on PBS, your old and beloved clothes, emails to your friends and family.

If you play this four-week game, consider keeping a short journal of your experiences. We expect you'll enjoy yourself. We don't mean to suggest that you'll achieve perfect happiness by living life without luxury. You'll miss some of the color, magic, and pleasure of human existence. Let's face it, buying luxuries can provide significant joy—think antique furniture, TiVo, the world's most beautiful art, the thrill of an unnecessary vacation in New Zealand. The Motley Fool is not an advocate of rendering life joyless in order to obsessively preserve cash.

The question is, how much of it will you miss?

And what luxury might you have been buying that is actually of little value to you?

Prove to yourself that you can tighten the purse string for a single month and see what comes of it. You may find you've been needlessly spending piles of cash on luxuries that deliver little pleasure. The way to find out is to live one month simply and see what you miss.

#3. THE "GARDNER CONSUMPTION THEORY" GAME

One way to make those spending changes is to carry The Motley Fool with you whenever you shop. How? By mastering a theory we've been blending in the beakers and Bunsen burners of Fool Labs.

It goes something like this:

America's greatest investors—Buffett, Getty, Rockefeller—have often said they succeeded by trying to buy a dollar of assets for just fifty cents. They wanted to pay half the value of businesses and properties when they invested. They wanted to buy a stock at half what they thought was its fair price. They wanted twice the reward for every investment.

That got us to thinking, "Why wouldn't such a theory work in *all* purchasing decisions?" After all, whenever we spend a dollar, we make an investment; we acquire an asset. That dollar might buy us a lottery ticket (which, on average, will pay us back only fifty cents). It might buy a cup of tea, or a fractional slice of a plane ticket to Dublin, or a larger investment in shares of a growing business.

If you can accept the suggestion that every dollar spent is a dollar invested, and that you should aspire to be like Warren Buffett, then you've largely grasped the game we've played for some time. It demands that you pay prices equal to no more than one half of a product's real value to you long-term. Sounds simple enough. How about the application? That's a little more difficult. How, after all, do you put a value on a bottle of Evian water or a tennis racket or new bookshelves for the study?

Not so easy.

In response, we echo Oscar Wilde: "Nowadays people know the prices of everything and the value of nothing." Think about it. How often do we place a value on a particular object before considering its price? Rarely. Given the statistics on consumer overspending in America, yes, rarely. We've assembled a simple mathematical approach for determining value. The equation is:

$$3x + 4 \sim 9g + [16r^\wedge 6xc] = V \text{ (where V is value)}$$

Got it?

Just plug in numbers for the variables, carry the equation through, and you'll know precisely the worth of all things. Jot down the equation on an index card, fold it in your wallet, and pull it out whenever you can't remember.

All right, now skip the nonsense.

Determining values in your life is a lot simpler: Double the price tag of anything you're buying. Then ask yourself, "Would I pay that (doubled) price for it?" If your answer is no, then the object in question isn't important enough to invest in. We suggest you skip it.

If the answer is yes, invest. Buy it.

Gardner Consumption Theory asks whether the following items are worth your investment:

GCT APPLIED		
ITEM IN QUESTION	LIST PRICE	YOUR PRICE?
Simon and Garfunkel CD	$12.95	$25.90
Vacation house	$200,000	$400,000
Hershey's chocolate bar	$0.52	$1.04
New PING golf clubs	$775	$1,550
Miele vacuum cleaner	$499	$998
This book (in hardcover)	$25.00	$50.00

We leave the answers to you. Will you derive twice the value of the price you pay? As you make your way through America's smorgasbord for consumers, double the price of everything and ask yourself, "Will I truly get lifetime value out of this product or service at this GCT price?" If you buy products and services as Rockefeller or Getty or Buffett bought stocks, you'll restrict your buying to items worth twice their listed price.

The upshot? You can expect to find yourself buying less, owning fewer half-used things, having cleaner closets, and deriving increased pleasure from what you choose to own. Try it, even just once in the mall, and experience a change.

#4. THE "BEAT BACK THE MAN" GAME

You've kept your receipts for a month. You've lived four weeks like a Spartan. You've forced an investor's mind-set onto your purchasing decisions. Now it's time to get The Man off your back. It is time to rid yourself of credit-card debt, once and for all.

Credit cards today carry an average interest rate of 15 percent per year. There is no investment—not real estate, not the stock market, not gold coins or corn futures—that can consistently outperform the 15 percent rates that banks charge you for short-term credit. Credit-card providers are among the most profitable ventures in American history. Why? Because they charge rates that exceed the possible returns of any investment available on this planet. Cardholders who don't pay their bills each month are giving credit-card companies returns they could not earn anywhere else.

You know the mathematical disaster that is unpaid credit-card debt. Yes? If you find yourself carrying short-term debt from month to month, it's time to blueprint more than a Spartan month; you may need to live a Spartan year or two. At Fool.com, our community has helped couples pay down as much as $60,000 in high-interest credit-card debt.

How do you play this game?

(1) Simplify your life to necessities and low-cost fun.
(2) Make the repayment of debts carrying interest rates of 10 percent or higher your *top* financial priority.

(3) Call and negotiate down interest rates on all your credit cards.

(4) Pay off the cards with the highest interest rates first.

(5) Along the way, create rewards for meeting debt payments.

(6) Before buying any luxury that costs more than $50, ask yourself if it'll matter to you in a year.

(7) Get the entire family involved in the game of saving and reward.

A lot of that may not sound like fun, but there's no clearer financial imperative than the need to pay down debt with double-digit interest rates. You can't save, earn your independence from financial worry, and freely pursue your goals in life if you're carrying unpaid credit-card debt from month to month. Pay it down, and never let it rise again.

Beat back The Man.

#5. THE "ONE FOR ME, NINE FOR YOU" GAME

Henceforth, for every dollar you make or inherit, set aside at least ten cents for your final two decades on earth. For every dime, set aside a penny. And as your salary increases, you should be putting away 20 percent or more (with a large salary) for your future.

There are countless places to put your money. We cover them in the next chapter, but how about a preview? You could invest your senior tithe in the Total Stock Market and Total Bond Market index funds from Vanguard. They would likely earn you your highest after-tax return. But maybe you want to enjoy your savings money while it appreciates. Clearly, that doesn't mean buying new cars and watching their value depreciate at 10 to 20 percent per year. It doesn't mean putting additions on your home that will never earn you a reward. (Hey, it's fine to put uneconomical additions on your home, but don't call that saved money.) It certainly doesn't mean spending your way around the globe. Might make for an outstanding life, just don't call it money saved for your future.

No, if you want to enjoy your investment money, then you'll want to consider a second home or multiple apartments across the country and world. You can earn rates of return that beat inflation; you may be able to rent them out; and you'll be able to enjoy these haunts at your leisure. Boston in the fall. New Orleans in the winter. Provence in the spring. Nova Scotia in the summer. A couple in their fifties with a dozen years of earning power could take out extended mortgages on apartments in all four of those spots. They could rent them for nine months out of the year, living in each for three months. With discount airlines popping up all over the place, the couple could preorder flights and fly on the cheap. Those mortgages *do* count as savings for the long term, because real estate appreciates with time.

However you choose to invest, absorb the key rule of this game: *One for your future for every nine you spend today.*

#6. THE "HOUSE THAT SAM WALTON BUILT" GAME

Sam Walton was the founder of Wal-Mart, the superstore that sells everything. His fortune has spread billions upon billions of dollars throughout the Walton family. Game number six is about turning your home into Sam's place.

Here's how.

First, get online.

Many Fools who've found us through our syndicated newspaper column or our NPR show are still not linked to the Internet. In our opinion, they should be. The variety of deals, the convenience of buying via Amazon.com, the mother lode of information makes the Internet a necessity for people of all ages. (Our ninety-two-year-old grandmother was an Internet user in the final years of her life.) At our website (www.Fool.com), you can get answers to virtually any financial question you can dream up.

So what does all that have to do with Sam Walton and your house?

Well, you can also make up for any overspending in your life by signing on to www.ebay.com. The worldwide auction site allows you to list your belongings for sale online. Old sporting equipment. The chaise lounge in the living room. Six pairs of blue jeans. The overload of crystal bowls from your wedding twenty-five years ago. Antique dining room chairs. A used automobile. Flowerpots. The coin collection. Your framed photo and autograph of General Dwight D. Eisenhower.

FOR FURTHER THINKING

Everyone makes financial mistakes; you will, too.
Here's the CEO of Elvis Presley Enterprises, Jack Soden,
on his dumbest business decision:

We licensed a company that made bedroom slippers. They were big, furry slippers, and they had this rubber image of Elvis's head on the toes. . . . When you saw those things in the store, you just kind of wondered, "What were we thinking?" David Letterman ended up wearing a pair on his show one night, and of course we pulled the license and got it off the market as fast as we could . . . and those slippers have gone on to become highly sought-after collector's items. These slippers go for like $1,000 on eBay, so what can I tell you?

It will take a day of research to understand how to list and sell on eBay. But you've been accumulating stuff for decades. So, think eBay (or have a yard sale). Listing for sale online what you don't need anymore can raise potentially thousands of dollars in new savings, which can then be invested. Your belongings will likely lose value with time; your invested savings will gain value with time.

If you're anything like the average American, your home is a mini Wal-Mart, a Sam Walton house. So, put those closets on sale! And then sock away that money—don't go out and spend it.

#7. THE "LIFE IS A CAR DEALERSHIP" GAME

We have an active member of The Motley Fool Community who's done a rather remarkable thing throughout his adult life: He has negotiated freely for anything and everything, turning retail America into one big car dealership. Early on, he mapped out the difference between necessities and luxuries in his life. He then resigned himself to paying the list price for anything he truly needed. But that opened the door on negotiating for anything he'd label a luxury.

What does the list include? Among many other things:

- airplane tickets
- hotel rooms
- compact discs
- new clothes
- computers
- furniture
- eating out
- books
- theater tickets
- jewelry
- kitchen supplies
- golf clubs

Throughout his life, he has bartered his way to a small fortune in savings. How? Whenever he didn't truly need something, he'd either ask for a special deal or offer to pay 10 to 40 percent less than the list price. Because these items weren't necessities, he was willing to walk if the retailer didn't make him a compelling offer. The keys to successful negotiating are: (a) the courage to go for it and (b) the ability to accept rejection with a twinkle in your eye.

Why might the game of negotiating for luxuries work? Because American retailers are awash in unsold inventory. Airliners fly with unused seats. Hotels have empty rooms. Clothing retailers display a slew of suits and shirts. All of these businesses have product to move, particularly in the midst of any recession. Yet they still often carry hefty markups.

With a keen eye for inventory overloads and willing managers, our negotiator lives well at a significant discount. He doesn't merely shop the sales; he creates them. He makes offers below the retail price on stuff he does not urgently need (which is most of what we buy in life). He gleefully accepts rejection. And, with a spring in his step, he enjoys anything from shallow to deep discounts on a wide variety of products.

Are we saying everyone's a great negotiator? No. Perhaps you're too embarrassed to try this, or you don't think you have the right stuff. For us, it's enough to point out The Possibility. *The Possibility,* at the very least. Many don't realize it exists.

We said our eight games get progressively more challenging or onerous. You can see that game number seven isn't always easy or pleasant (although it can be made very pleasant). But, hey, it's your future we're fighting for here. If you're looking into a retirement fund that seems inadequate, or if you have debts to pay, why not at least consider negotiating on nonnecessities for a month and see what comes of it?

If you can't stomach a life of negotiation, at least shop the discounts, clip coupons, and use the discount warehouses (such as Costco and Wal-Mart) to your advantage. Your savings invested today are your comfortable retirement tomorrow.

#8. THE "DOUBLE TIME FOR DOUBLE MUCH" GAME

At the end of our list of savings opportunities is your decision to sign up for a second job. This is the least appealing game of all.

Wouldn't it be far better to design a budget, live a relatively Spartan life, eliminate credit-card debt, save 10 to 20 percent of your take-home pay, sell your leftover belongings on eBay, and smilingly negotiate discounts? Probably. But in some cases, all of that enterprise won't be enough to carry the day.

It's time for a second job.

As you will read throughout our book, our idea of a good job is any work you enjoy. That goes for your core job, but the principle is doubly important if you take on a second job. The greater your financial need, the less demanding you can afford to be. But each of us can steer toward labor that plays off talents and natural interests. Furthermore, when we work at what we love (whether it's waiting tables, fixing people's computers, flight instructing, or providing medical care), the work is hardly labor. Some of America's greatest entrepreneurs have put in fifteen-hour-plus workdays long after earning their millions, long after their business made the textbooks.

Why?

Because they had obsessive-compulsive workaholism?

Actually, most of them didn't.

Most of them simply *worked at what they loved.*

A second job could earn you anything in excess of ten thousand dollars in annual take-home pay. It's not our first choice for supplementing savings—it's our eighth. But it is a very practical, if tiring, way to juice your financial plan as you head into retirement.

Conclusion

These are our eight games for saving money. If you choose to play, and you earn anything north of $30,000 a year, these games should help you save in excess of $2,000 each year.

Note that we've framed them as *games* because we firmly believe they should be played in that spirit. They should be inclusive, involving your spouse and your kids. And, as always, good games are about winning. You have the rules you need to know. You've probably already been forming some strategies.

Now win them.

Action Plan

■ Play the games in this chapter. For starters, solve your one-month mystery. Track all your expenses for a month and sort them into necessities and luxuries. See what you learn and what changes you're inspired to make.

■ Next month try living a Spartan life. Spend money only on absolute necessities, like your mortgage payment, utilities, groceries, etc. See which luxuries you miss and which you don't.

■ Beat back The Man. Dig your way out of credit-card debt—and let us help you with that, too, with some strategies and tips. (Drop by www.Fool.com/ccc.)

■ If you're a wee bit weary of financial games, treat yourself to some new nonfinancial games. Discover the world of modern family-strategy games, which our families have enjoyed for many years. You can read about many and order some at www.Funagain.com. Try Lost Cities, Wyatt Earp, Settlers of Catan, Evo, Carcassonne, Bohnanza, and Zertz. (But get back to your all-important finances later, okay?)

Chapter Six

Investing Now Versus Then

You can never plan the future by the past.
—EDMUND BURKE

"INVESTING NOW VERSUS THEN" is an apt title, because Now and Then are satisfyingly ambiguous. This is a chapter primarily about how to invest when you're past forty ("now") versus how you may have invested prior to forty ("then"). In the meantime, the market has gone through such a huge rise, followed by a nearly unprecedented fall, that "Now Versus Then" has another important meaning, too—about what lessons one can learn from a volatile investment environment. We're going to stay focused on the former meaning, but the latter will no doubt intrude at points.

In previous Motley Fool books, we've emphasized the stock market. If you've read any (or all!!!) of them, you know that we teach two basic approaches.

The first is to buy an index fund that effectively puts you into from five hundred to more than five thousand stocks so that you *are* the stock market. You own practically all the stocks! All that for a very low fee, which is the key to a good index fund. Take something like the low-fee Vanguard Total Stock Market Index Fund (VTSMX) or S&P Depository Receipts (AMEX: SPY), and you have your stock investment right there, offering you total diversification. Your challenges are to add to it, to not check in too often, and to get on with your life.

The second approach is to select individual stocks. This requires more knowledge, risk-taking, and sangfroid, and with those come more fun, more learning, and potentially much greater rewards. As anyone can see from our past work, we love to write about individual stocks. If you, too, are a fan and are looking for more than what this book provides, we have our own market-beating investment newsletter, called "The Motley Fool Stock Advisor," available for annual subscription (call for a sample toll-free, 1-888-665-FOOL). We love the opportunity we have in this country to buy individual stocks of amazing corporations, great and small.

With this book, our focus isn't on selecting a good mix of individual stocks. Nope. "Investing Now Versus Then" is about ASSET ALLOCATION. We put that in all caps because we need to begin to appreciate and celebrate the concept of ASSET ALLOCATION when we're over forty.

If you have any interest in or knowledge about investing, you've probably heard this term before, perhaps quite often. It refers to the mix of investment types you choose for your money. The simplest way to think about it is stocks versus bonds versus cash.

Traditionally, we have urged investors to put into the stock market any long-term-savings money, defined as money you won't need for at least five years, at a minimum. Why? Because the stock market has historically returned an average of 10 to 11 percent per year, well outpacing virtually all other asset classes, including the 7 to 8 percent on bonds and the marginally better returns on real estate. The market's volatility is a fact, and it must become an accepted fact by the patient and Foolish investor. But that general advice continues to be just as compelling to us, despite the horrible early-twenty-first-century sell-off, which arguably makes the advice better and timelier these days.

This advice *loses effectiveness* the further we get beyond forty, however. At forty, you still have twenty-five years until retirement. We think you should still maintain a serious and focused allocation in stocks. But as time passes, we are increasingly managing money less for so-called capital appreciation and more for capital *preservation*. Those lump-sum payments coming from your retirement or pension plans—those things, combined with Social Security, may be all you have to live on! Taking undue investment risk isn't appropriate. You don't have the same luxury of time to recover from economic or financial downturns that you did in your salad days when you were green. If you've left formal employment, presumably you wish to keep it that way—no more formal employment.

It's about Investing Now, not Then.

FOCUS ON WORK YEARS LEFT, NOT AGE

Loads of advice for boomer investing suggests subtracting your age from 110, with the remainder being the percentage you should have in stocks. So if you're 51 years old, 110 minus 51 equals 59, which suggests you should have 59 percent of your investments in stocks. We have advised this in the past, and it's not wrong or bad advice.

However, we believe it's more helpful to ask not how old you are but rather how much longer you expect to be working, in order to figure out allocation of your assets. Rather than focusing on your age, we're going to think through how to allocate your money based on your expected work years remaining.

Fifteen-plus Years
The further you are from ceasing formal employment, the more of your money should be in stocks. Please keep in mind that in approximately 90 percent of all five-year periods over the last century (1901–1906, 1902–1907, etc.), the stock market has been a better place to have your money than a standard passbook savings account. Given this, what's the right allocation in stocks, and for what periods?

Well, even after a bad bear market—or perhaps *especially,* given the recent bad bear market—we continue to think that you should maximize the percentage of your assets in stocks for your long-term account. We feel comfortable saying that if you have fifteen or more years before expected retirement, *you should consider allocating 100 percent of your investable assets in the stock market—*

as represented by the Vanguard Total Stock Market Index Fund or S&P Depositary Receipts.

Your expected averaged return is 9 to 11 percent. You can do the math to see how your long-term portfolio value will ramp up. Here's an exercise worth trying: Take the total starting value of your retirement portfolio and multiply it by 1.10 (10 percent annual growth) over and over, once for every year you'll keep your money invested and reinvested. You're compounding your returns, multiplying by 1.1 the full amount reached in the previous year. The result is just an estimate of what your portfolio may look like, but it's often eye-opening for those who have never done it before—either to see how big those numbers can get (if you have lots of time) or to see how non-big those numbers get (if you have less).

Who, with fifteen years or more to invest before retiring, *shouldn't* invest 100 percent in the amazingly diversified world of stocks brought to you by Vanguard's Total Stock Market Index Fund? Answer: anyone who doesn't feel comfortable with stocks overall, their volatility in particular. There are indeed many who can't stand watching their retirement money fluctuate by swings of 20 percent or more, up or down over a given year. Some people can't even stomach a 30 percent rise! We understand. You want stability.

What to Do if Stocks Aren't Right for You
If this seems to describe you, let us suggest one of two possibilities.

First, you can downshift into a safer but still growth-oriented portfolio of 60 percent in stocks and 40 percent in bonds. That asset allocation is dependable, even for those more advanced in age who are relying on their investment portfolio for year-to-year subsistence. We mentioned in Chapter 3 that over the past century, this 60/40 allocation has produced an annualized return of about 8.75 percent, with less gut-wrenching year-to-year changes than the stock market overall. But keep in mind you are still invested over half in stocks, so you are not immune. Again the timeless rule that cannot be avoided, try as one might: Reward correlates with risk. This 8.75 percent return, far preferable to "mailing it in" with a basic savings or CD interest rate, isn't achieved risk-

or heartache-free. You will occasionally suffer, but over your chosen fifteen-plus-year period, you will probably wind up happy with your decision. You can even transition increasing amounts of your money into a bond ladder as time passes, which we'll explain later.

It's worth reiterating that this option will, in most fifteen-plus-year market periods, net you less of a return than the 100 percent stock allocation—often far less. Realize you're consciously forgoing bigger gains.

That's approach number one for those who don't like risk.

For number two, let us introduce you to a new fund for your consideration: the Vanguard Balanced Index Fund (VBINX). What is "balanced" about it? Its ratio of stocks to bonds. As of this writing, VBINX sported a ratio of—get this—61 percent stocks (mostly large companies, the average such company worth $28 billion) to 39 percent bonds (with an average maturity—length of term—of a rather conservative 7.2 years, invested in highly rated fixed-income securities). The historic return of this fund (opened in 1992) was, as of this writing, 8.63 percent.

If these figures look eerily similar to scenario number one, your eyes do not deceive you. Vanguard's "balanced" answer mimics the 60/40 allocation put forth in option number one—the very same allocation that repeated studies have shown efficiently balances growth with safety over the long term. The Vanguard fund does give you one-stop shopping, particularly convenient for those who have it in their 401(k) or IRA plans. The annual expense ratio was, at last check, only 0.22 percent (a full percentage point lower per year than the fees carried by the average mutual fund in America).

Finally, note what Vanguard itself says about this fund on its own website: "Who Should Not Invest: Investors unwilling to accept significant fluctuations in share price."

For those investing fifteen or more years prior to retirement, those are words best respected and acknowledged but not allowed to curtail too severely a willingness to invest and take risk. You have years until you'll use this money. Keep it staked in higher-risk arenas, and you'll likely be far better off when you're eating cake at your own send-off party.

FIVE TO FIFTEEN

For those planning to leave the traditional workforce within a decade, give or take five years, you need to take a different perspective. The biggest question you have to answer is "How much risk can I *afford* to take or do I want to take?" If you have more than enough money to retire on, above-average risk tolerance, or both, you can keep pretty fully invested in stocks. Particularly for those who'll be working for a decade or more, you can tend to follow the advice in the preceding subsection.

By contrast, if you are closer to five years from quitting work, or if you are carefully approaching the "right" amount of money to achieve financial independence, you should be loath to sacrifice your hard work and planning to a potentially poor stock market. We know we don't have to work too hard to convince you that over a short-term period of a few years, the market can get killed! Therefore, if the first sentence of this paragraph describes you, invest accordingly. The Vanguard Balanced Index Fund should be perhaps your most aggressive form of investment. More appropriate for many will be the greater safety and lower returns of the bond market.

Vanguard (you've heard us mention them before, eh?) comes to the rescue with another fine fund, this also sporting just a 0.22 percent annual fee. The fund is the Vanguard Total Bond Market Index Fund (VBMFX). Now over fifteen years old, VBMFX has returned about 7.8 percent annually since its inception, through bond markets good and bad. It is a safe option for those nearing and in retirement. It gives you diversification across many types of bonds and beats inflation's 3 percent historical drag.

You have other options. In fact, Vanguard has several different bond funds, including long-term, intermediate-term, and short-term (safest) bond index funds. And you can buy your own bonds, which we will, as promised, cover below.

If you're not finding an emphatic one-size-fits-all suggestion here, that's because you need to decide for yourself what might be the best mix based on your *time till retirement* and your *risk tolerance*. Mixes of 60 percent stocks and 40 percent bonds are quite common, particularly for those a decade away from life without regular work. Some will maintain a near 100 percent balance in the stock market, especially those who can afford to do so because they have extra time or lots of money ("lots of money" defined as "even if it loses substantial value, you remain financially independent").

On the other hand, some who are five years from making regular work an increasingly distant memory—specifically those who have lost faith in stocks, following the worst market since the Great Depression—may go 100 percent in short-term bond funds. Vanguard's Short-Term Bond Index Fund (VBISX) has returned 6.5 percent since its 1994 debut, which included a 7.9 percent annualized return during the extended stock-market crash of 2000–2002. Not too shabby. Definitely one of your safer options, providing you with more predictability than most plans.

Before going to our "Five Years and In" subsection, may we interject a primary point?

Thank you, we will.

KEEP THINGS SIMPLE!

Cast a skeptical eye at any financial advisor who makes complicated suggestions. Complicating your investments is a quick way to lose touch with them. The proposals we've made above, and indeed throughout all Motley Fool literature, are intended to be useful because of their simplicity and convenience and ease of execution.

The word "risk" is inescapable when it comes to transforming your cash into other assets, whether international bond funds or a single domestic stock, such as Wal-Mart. You should keep any dollar you care about invested in something you understand. The risks that end up hurting us are those we never understood in the first place and didn't factor in as true risks. This happens when we operate outside our own zone of comfort.

So we ask you to swear to yourself:

I will keep things simple, investing only when I understand the upside and downside of whatever I'm doing.

Speaking of not understanding what you're doing, history is littered most of all with the wreckage of those who saw only the upside.

FOR FURTHER THINKING

George Foreman on his dumbest investment:

David: George, our radio show is about investing and money, and we frequently feature people who are well known, and they tell us looking back over their lives their smartest and their dumbest investments.

George Foreman: Oh boy. I can tell you the dumbest. The price of cattle was skyrocketing back in the middle '70s. So I invested, I mean, hundred thousands more than you could ever guess into the cattle business. The bottom fell out quick. They were worth ten cents overnight.

Tom: How much did you lose?

Foreman: I think at that time about $700,000, which is the equivalent of $2 million today.

Okay, back to our time intervals.

FIVE YEARS AND IN

Congratulations that you find yourself within five years of hanging up your spikes (felicitous baseball expression). Many never reach anything like financial independence, even including Social Security. Looks like you're almost there.

First of all, we need to make sure you have the cash reserves suitable for your new life. *Try to cover two years' worth of living expenses with a straight investment into money-market funds.* These ultrasafe investments aren't going to do anything more exciting than ensure that you have enough to weather any unexpected storms. Two years' full expenses amassed and collecting interest is exactly the answer. If you have a very large retirement (i.e., if you are quite rich), then to be safe, put up to 10 percent of your wealth in that money market, even if that figure comes to over two years of living expenses. That's the conservative thing, and we'd do it in your position.

With cash reserves put away and ready, as you approach the nonworking portion of your adult life (may it be longer than the working portion), you're left deciding again how your remainder should be invested.

Let's pretend you're going to live another twenty years. Safe bet, we hope.

How do you imagine you should invest? We saw a trend above: The less time you have till retirement, the less risk you should take. Does that mean that those who are practically already retired should, in their last few work years or months, put the money in a locked chest in their basement?

Actually, no. If you have two years of expenses set aside in money markets, we suggest you invest it as explained in the previous subsection—the five- to fifteen-year approach. You are advised to be more conservative as you get closer to retirement day.

So why the overall similarity in approach to those who still have five to fifteen years to invest for retirement? Because if you go *too* conservative—too much for income and not enough for growth— you may run out of funds, if you live a long time, as your investments may fail to keep up with inflation.

Of course, you retain a wide variety of options.

You may wish to maintain a bond portfolio using the Vanguard Total Bond Market Index Fund, fueled by its impressive 5 percent annual yield. Or, as you will discover in Chapter 15, you may want to maintain that 60/40 ratio *throughout* your days, if and when humanly possible. Doing so ensures—to say it once again— that you have a good income stream that will also grow enough to track or outpace inflation.

There you have it. Asset allocation from 100 percent in stocks for those with miles to go before they get to sleep (and sleep *late, every day,* if your body will let you, and ah, the wonder of it . . . it does sound nice) right down to those for whom this present year is the last they'll ever take a salary check. We've tried to keep things simple and useful.

BUYING INDIVIDUAL STOCKS

For the purposes of this chapter, we've assumed you want to choose index funds. It's the correct choice for most of us, since we usually don't want to get too complicated or caught up in details.

That said, the stock market may be a particular passion or great interest of yours. You may already be substituting individual stocks for the equities portions considered in this chapter's allocations, or you may wish to do so in the future. Wonderful. We teach lots about individual stock investing in our book *The Motley Fool Investment Guide.* We also provide stock picks in our newsletters "The Motley Fool Stock Advisor," "The Motley Fool Hidden Gems," and "The Motley Fool Income Investor."

If you do like the idea of *some* stocks, you don't have to go whole hog. For whatever your desired percentage of stock allocation, you could buy an index fund with half of that and invest the other half in individual securities. *Be incremental.* We italicize this because we frequently find ourselves saying it, in the face of so many who seem to think money decisions are binary—yes or no, all or none, now or later. To return to baseball one more time, it's okay to hit singles or doubles, stopping on first or second base. Being incremental, you'll probably still reach home and score. The decision should *not* be between hitting a home run or not picking up a bat at all.

Be incremental.

NOT ALL STOCKS ARE CREATED EQUAL

When you buy a diversified stock index fund, you get a huge variety of companies. You have ball-bearing manufacturers right next to ritzy software firms. It's not Pepsi versus Coke; you own Pepsi *and* Coke. And a financial services firm, too. Dozens of them, in fact. It's not easy to wrap our human minds around the idea of owning five thousand different stocks, but in a total market index fund, that's what you own.

If you're planning to select individual stocks, you need to create some of that diversity yourself. That does not usually mean buying Pepsi to diversify away from Coke. Nope, you'll need to pick *between* those two for a strong, disciplined individual investor portfolio of eight to fifteen stocks. Or ignore these two altogether if your interests lie elsewhere.

Within the category of "stocks," there are two types that move quite independently of the overall market. Both are more conservative and less volatile than growth stocks. And both provide far more annual income through dividends than the average growth stock. So we figured we should bring your attention to them.

Our favorite of the two are REITs, or real estate investment trusts. These are businesses that wrap together numerous real estate properties into a single company, paying out, say, the rental fees for the properties in the form of annual dividends to shareholders. There are many different types of REITs, from hotels to health-care facilities and everything in between, making this a world unto itself. If you're interested in these investments, which perform near the market's historical averages but often move contrarily (i.e., they lose to the market in good years and beat up on the market in bad years), we highly suggest you pick up Motley Fool Community member Ralph Block's excellent book *Investing in REITs*. As an added bonus, Ralph is a longtime and active contributor to our discussion area at Fool.com, so if you read his book and have a question, you stand a decent chance of being able to ask him yourself. (Point your browser to http://boards.fool.com and, after registering, locate the "Real Estate & REITs" discussion board in the Industry and Market Analysis folder. If you have any problems finding it, just email our customer service at CS@Fool.com.)

Anyway, not to be distracted by the primary point, REITs are a very nice alternative investment that can flatten out volatility for those for whom flattened-out volatility is a goal. And they pay very high dividends, often exceeding 5 percent yields (in effect, interest rates) per year.

A second category of stocks that don't behave like "normal" stocks are utilities. We don't have quite so much enthusiasm to share with you here, since the utilities industry is both highly regulated and not as stable as it once was. However, saying that it's not as stable as it once was is kind of like saying Frank Sinatra is not as popular as he once was—the truth is that he's still very popular and well regarded as a crooner, and most utilities are still pretty darn safe. Utilities traditionally have lower annual returns than REITs but are more predictable and pay comparable dividends. If you're interested in owning some stocks directly—you're why we're writing this little section—at least factor these into your thinking, however many you buy or don't buy.

FOR FURTHER THINKING

Tennis star Billie Jean King's smartest and dumbest investments:

Billie Jean King: The dumbest investments were the dot-coms, but I knew this was a dumb investment and I didn't care. I like entrepreneurial people. I like people who take risks. I know that is where I take my "fun mon," and I put it in, and if I get lucky in one out of a hundred, great. If I don't, so be it. If I hit a couple of singles and maybe one home run in a lifetime, great. But my smartest one, as far as being the most fun, has been my World Team Tennis Professional League. Putting money back into our business has been the right thing to do, and I want to put money back into tennis because it has been so good to me.

HOW TO MAINTAIN THE PERCENTAGES

Saying that you should maintain a 60/40 allocation between stocks and bonds prompts the question "How." After all, you may *start* with 60/40, but all of a sudden, in your very first year, the stock market rises 18 percent and the bond market stays flat. You were only minding your own business, but you find yourself out of whack at the end of the year, overloaded in stocks.

A balanced index fund like Vanguard's does this for you—another reason we like that option. But many of us have more than one investment, so here are a few helpful tips.

You have three primary options. The first is the most obvious: To restore the balance, sell investments in which you're overweighted and redeploy the right amount of money to investments in which you're underweighted. We would recommend you do this not more than once a year, if that, and do it with a clear understanding of the tax implications. Consult www.irs.gov or a tax advisor.

The second way to achieve rebalancing, which is preferable to the first if it'll do the job for you, is to take new money (income savings, inheritance, etc.) and invest it where you're underweighted. Obviously, if new savings are not sufficient, some combination of the other options may be necessary.

A third way: Instead of automatically reinvesting dividends and interest, have that money deposited together in one place—typically in a money-market account or other single obvious place of safekeeping. Then, when it comes time to buy more stocks or bonds (depending), use the money already acquired as income from your bonds or stocks to reestablish your desired allocation. By channeling all income generation to one account, you also make your year-end accounting much easier come tax time.

Further or more serious tweaks may be necessary from time to time but don't generally need to be considered more than once a year, if that. If you are dealing in any more complexity than this, or if you are shifting large amounts, talk to a tax advisor.

THE LADDER IS NOT JUST FOR CHANGING LIGHTBULBS

Both bonds and CDs, in most economic environments, give you higher interest rates and greater potential returns the longer you're willing to lock up your money (considered a greater risk). But when you want to invest in bonds and CDs, you're often initially forced to spread out your maturity dates from short-term to long-term to limit risk.

Enter *ladders*, which aren't just for changing lightbulbs anymore. Ladders help you smooth your diversified assets into longer- and higher-yielding investments.

Let's take a bond ladder as an example.

Once you know how much you want to commit to bonds in percentage terms and translate that to real dollars, you need to get invested. You could load it all into one ten-year bond, earn a set amount of interest every year, and get your principal back ten years later, all at once, to be reinvested. But what if you need some of the money in the meantime? Maybe you need to spend it, or maybe you need to sell some off to invest in stocks and rebalance your allocations.

The answer is to buy bonds with different maturities.

Let's say you split up your money in five different allotments, buying a one-year bond, a two-year, a three-year, a five-year, and a ten-year bond. At the end of the first year, in addition to the interest you'll get paid by all five, your one-year will come due and return your principal investment. Now, with that money, *buy a new ten-year bond.* You have now deployed two fifths of your money in ten-year bonds, and they'll come due at different times as well. You will slowly move from two fifths of your bond money in ten-year bonds to *five* fifths, thanks to constant ongoing use of the ladder. By rinsing and repeating, you'll have regular money coming back every year and at a higher (longer-term) interest rate than you would have achieved by reinvesting your money at whatever the short-term rate du jour is.

Ladders help smooth out the risk of your interest rates going too low. Murphy's Law dictates that this will happen at the very worst time you need to reinvest. If you have all your money loaded into one investment and you've carried an 8 percent interest rate for a couple of decades, you'll have to reinvest it at 5 percent. And that can be catastrophic. With a ladder this doesn't happen.

Please note: The same process can and should be used with CDs.

What's the fee cost of this approach?

Scott Burns of *The Dallas Morning News* points out, "If you have one [bond] renewal a year and purchase a new issue through a broker the total cost will be $50 a year or less. *That's 1/10 of one percent on a $100,000 portfolio* [italics ours]. In addition, interest on Treasury obligations is not subject to state income taxes, a boon for residents of high-tax states."

Action Plan

■ Spend some time mulling over your asset allocation. Given your age, retirement plans, temperament, and other factors, do you have too much of your money sitting in stocks, bonds, or something else? Should you park some money in laddered CDs? Determine what mix would be best for you and what you're comfortable with. Then take steps to rejigger your holdings.

■ Learn more about real estate investment trusts (REITs) and consider whether they deserve a spot in your portfolio. You can learn all about REITs at www.nareit.com and in Ralph Block's *Investing in REITs*.

■ Pat yourself on the back now for addressing all these important issues that so many people perpetually ignore. Treat yourself, too—perhaps call an old friend to reconnect. (In the spirit of this book, though, at least consider calling collect!)

Chapter Seven

Financial Advisors
Better Than Dogs

Dogs, ye have had your day!
—ALEXANDER POPE

WE BEGAN THIS section of the book asking, "What Is Enough, and for How Long?" We provided you a ready framework for considering the question, and have since tried to fill out the picture by focusing on ways to *increase* and *invest* your savings. In certain cases, though, answering "What Is Enough, and for How Long?" may introduce greater and greater complexities. Or perhaps you're not someone ready or willing to practice Emersonian self-reliance. Good news: There's help if you need it. The key first consideration is actually finding help, as opposed to someone else's greedy self-interest masquerading as help.

Consider the following two scenarios—neither of which, by the way, has anything to do with dogs.

Scenario #1: It's the end of December, and as you're shopping for stocking stuffers, you consider the gift of college savings for your kids. Is there anything you should do before the calendar year ends? You decide to consult a financial planner who, after explaining her fee structure, asks you lots of questions about the black-and-white financial aspects of your life and then delves into some of your less tangible money wishes for the future. Using the information you've given her, she prints out various college savings scenarios and specific account options, including fees, and advantages and disadvantages. She tells you that you have a few weeks to make a decision based on this fiscal year, and advises you to take a little time to review your options. She also notes a few year-end tax moves that would be advantageous.

Scenario #2: It's the end of December, and as you stand in a line thirty deep at Target, your thoughts turn to money. You decide to seek the help of a financial advisor to see if your savings are on track. You pass his attractive and amiable assistant and enter a distinguished office—leather wingback chairs flanked by framed certificates summarizing his credentials, with artistic flourishes all 'round. You relax; *this is the place.* Moments after you enter his office, he begins a cautionary tale about the ravages the health-care system can have on finances. He recommends that you purchase a whole-life policy before the roads ice over. Oh, and while reviewing your finances, he notices what he considers to be a subpar mutual fund in your portfolio. How about, instead, his firm's Selective Large-Cap Balanced Fund (i.e., the Overpriced Fat-Cat Fund)? Sure, you say. You don't want to be stuck with a bum fund when it comes time to retire. Of course, he doesn't tell you right then that his mutual fund has a front- and back-end load (if you even know what those are), and that he gets a nice commission for selling it to you . . .

The right financial professional can make all the difference in your future quality of life. The wrong one can ruin it. (And we'll have more to say about dogs at the end.)

When to Hire a Pro

Reasons to hire a paid financial advisor run the gamut from building your initial plans as a twenty-four-year-old to making the best decision on your estate at the end of your life. Here are most of the common scenarios in which we recommend you at least consider independent professional help.

Complex financial products. Automobile insurance, or term life, is generally simple enough that most motivated adults can find the best (and cheapest!) product either by asking around or, preferably, using the Internet. But what about complex products, like disability and long-term care insurance? And do you need an umbrella liability policy? One can certainly arrive at good answers to these and other challenges by doing one's own research (and we've dedicated Chapter 9 to health care). The question is, are you the sort who will?

Saving for college. It's the last day of the tax year, and you have a few pesos coming back. You want to make a contribution to a tax-sheltered college savings account for your kids. What are the pros and cons of all the options? Do you have to decide today? "Paying for Your Kids and College" (Chapter 12) will help, but some people need a little more handholding, especially if the situation is unusual or complicated.

Estate planning. It's not just about avoiding taxes. Have you thought about who will manage the kids' inheritance should you die unexpectedly? Do you want them controlling what's left of the life-insurance payout at age eighteen, or does a separate arrangement sound better? Should you set up a trust? We'll be happy to help in "Planning Your Estate" (Chapter 14), but our primary bit of advice is to seek the services of a professional (we'll tell you how to find the best one). You don't want to make a bad show of your last will and testament.

Sudden "retirement." Your employer has hit the skids, and you're being offered an early retirement package. Should you take it? Do you have enough money to retire? Perhaps four different brokers have shown you four different plans; two say you can retire, and two say you can't. Could you use an objective review?

Employee stock options. Should you exercise your employee stock options this year or next year? And what are the tax implications?

These are just a few examples. At The Motley Fool, for ten years we've met people online and offline who are seeking to make better financial decisions. In many cases, they just need to obtain the right bit of information or a proper viewpoint. Many of our members are motivated to succeed on their own in one or more areas of their financial lives. But many others are neither motivated nor equipped, or they may be capable in one area but not another. It is for this reason that we impress upon everyone the importance of seeking and insisting upon *independent* financial advice (that which does not come with commissions for salesmen and conflicts of interest within a firm). You should be seeking it whenever thousands of dollars or more are on the line, any situation in which a mistake would be costly—far more costly than an hour of consultation.

FOR FURTHER THINKING

Movie critic Roger Ebert on his favorite line about money:

Roger Ebert: You know, I think the funniest line of dialogue that David Mamet has ever written was about money. It comes in his movie *Heist*. Danny DeVito is trying to convince Gene Hackman to pull one more job. Gene Hackman says he really doesn't want to do it; he would rather go sailing. DeVito says, "You got to do it." Hackman says, "Why do I have to do it?" DeVito says, "For the money." Hackman says, "I don't need money." DeVito comes up with this classic Mamet line, which ought to be the motto of The Motley Fool: "Everybody needs money. That's why they call it 'money'!"

FINDING THE RIGHT FINANCIAL PRO

Did you marry the first person you kissed? Perhaps, but most of us kissed a few different people before we settled on whom to link our lives to. Similarly, the best approach to hiring a financial planner involves meeting more than one and screening carefully. You didn't screen if you hired the first person you met. Careful screening pays in relationships, but even more so in finance.

Thankfully, this process is made much easier by the key fact that any financial planner worth his or her salt will give you an hour of time free, up-front, both to explore your needs and to explain how he or she operates.

Now, a big chunk of this initial meeting will be devoted to establishing—in the planner's mind—a rough overview of your overall financial health. But you also want to leave plenty of time to evaluate a candidate and get a solid understanding of how the relationship will work: how often you'll meet, what the planner will and will not do, how well the planner answers tough questions, and *how the planner is paid*. We put that last bit in italics to flag how important it is to us. It's so important that we'll cover that in its own section, below.

Let it be said again: We Fools have always maintained that *you* are the best person to manage your money. After all, *you are the CEO of your own financial empire.* But like any successful executive, you'll occasionally need to seek expert advice. Given this, Mr. or Ms. CEO, wouldn't you want to make sure that the members of your team are all working for the best interests of you and your company? You wouldn't want to name a chief financial officer who had outside allegiances, or a head of corporate communications who had her own special causes that she would always try to jam into company press releases. When you're seeking advice, you want it to be independent and unconflicted, totally focused on the best long-term interests of your organization.

When it comes to taking financial advice, the situation is exactly the same. Remember that *you* are making all the decisions, *you* are accountable for them, and *you and only you* will most pointedly feel their effects. The only way to avoid conflicted or outright harmful advice is to become a more educated consumer. You need to be able to recognize a financial advisor's conflicts. You need to be able to see through someone else's agenda.

Financial advisors are the generalists of money management. A financial advisor (also referred to as a "planner," or "CFP," for certified financial planner) assesses your overall financial picture with an eye toward your retirement investments, savings, debts, insurance, and other big areas of your money life. Some planners are additionally equipped to offer estate-planning advice or input on your tax situation.

You may consider this surprising, but in most states anyone can call him- or herself a financial planner. There are no licensing requirements and very little regulation. But there are credentials and designations, and the following letters in today's alphabet soup are worth translating:

CFA—chartered financial analyst
CFP—certified financial planner

ChFC—chartered financial consultant
CPA—certified public accountant
MBA—masters of business administration
RIA—registered investment advisor
RR—registered representative

A good way to expose charlatan financial advisors is to note that they lack any of the above. Of course, credentials don't reveal actual talents or skill. Some can be easily attained in a matter of days, requiring minimal experience, others are extremely difficult to receive and take years of study. That's why it's helpful to seek individual referrals (from a friend, ideally, but third-party present or former customers of the advisor are worth checking as well). And remember that often the most important credential—experience—is overlooked.

If someone has been in business a decade or longer, that suggests a few good things. First, since he or she has been around the block a few times, you can fairly impute to the advisor a good base of both knowledge and experience working with clients. And second, since he or she has managed to stay in business that long, you can fairly infer that the advisor is good enough to have maintained good clients and a good business. Again, both of these are good things, and they highlight the importance of finding experienced advisors.

Let us not pass on to fees before pointing out that when it comes to hiring any kind of financial advisor, the more *you* know, the more effectively you can work with the pro.

ASK BEFORE YOU PAY

We stated above: "You need to be able to see through someone else's agenda." That's a good segue into paying your financial advisor, since *the single best way to understand any professional's motivation is to ask how he or she gets paid.* How a person is being compensated speaks eloquently about how she or he will perform for you. This doesn't come down to a "Honey, let's choose Sally, because her hourly advice is the most affordable" sort of price shopping. No. This comes down to motivation shopping, looking around insistently for service that will *benefit* you, service that is *designed* to benefit you, starting with exactly how and why the service giver is being paid. You can't overestimate the importance of this.

As we consider fees, remember first that not many worthwhile pros work for peanuts. Don't get so ruthless about cost that you end up with worthless advice. In so many contexts, it is repeatedly true that you get what you pay for in this world. However, it is also clear that in the financial world, more than perhaps any other sector of society, this axiom tends to break down with surprising frequency. Because of the nation's mainstream ignorance about money, we are by default opening the door for crummy or ill-motivated people to put big price tags on poor merchandise, selling their wares to naive people who don't know how to figure costs on mutual funds or what the benchmark performance of the stock market has been. But we still believe that you generally do get what you pay for.

Financial planners draw pay in one or more of four basic ways—many will mix and match.

COMMISSIONS
Commission payments come in three primary flavors:

- Onetime sales rewards, such as mutual-fund loads, or the up-front payments that come from selling annuities and cash-value life-insurance policies
- Ongoing service payments, such as annual commissions paid to insurance agents upon policy renewal
- Commissions paid for transactions, such as buying and selling shares of stock

FEES BASED ON PERCENTAGE OF ASSETS
Some planners charge a straight percentage of your total assets on an annual basis—either all assets (from your personal balance sheet) or just those they help you manage. This is the most common arrangement for paying an independent financial planner and is increasing in popularity.

FEE BASED ON AN HOURLY RATE

Under this arrangement, you do the bulk of the work and pay the planner for information and advice on an as-needed basis, like the typical arrangement with a lawyer.

FLAT FEE FOR A ONETIME FINANCIAL PLAN

You pay a hefty up-front fee—often in the many thousands of dollars—for a glossy write-up of your financial empire, complete with some recommendations for action.

As we already implied, these four ways to make a living are not mutually exclusive. In fact, the majority of financial planners are compensated by a combination of fees *and* commissions. It's important to know a bit about where a planner derives her paycheck. Here are numerous tips to help you weed through the gobbledygook:

(1) Don't be misled by simple labels. *Ask planner candidates exactly how they will be paid.* "Fee-only" should mean that the planner accepts no sales or trading commissions. *Ask directly to be sure.* Repeat the question if you're not clear about the answer.

(2) "Fee-based" and "fee-offset" are *not* the same as "fee-only." The fundamental basis of these relationships is a fee, but subsequent commissions are also part of the package—either charged on top of fees ("fee-based") or subtracted from fees ("fee-offset"). Needless to say, perhaps, but "fee-offset" for this reason is far better than "fee-based."

(3) Find somebody with whom you can develop a long-term relationship, even if you rarely seek advice. You don't want to start over again every time, especially if your next money problem comes with a tight time line.

(4) In the best case, even a well-intentioned commission-based planner might overlook the best option for you if he's untrained and gets paid to sell you a product. In the worst case, commission-only planners are thinly disguised salesmen with no interest at all in your finances—beyond selling you the one product for which they are most highly compensated.

(5) Unless you know exactly what you're after, stay away from the "complete financial plan for a few thousand dollars" option.

The results are often long on glossy charts but short on specific advice about solving your unique problems. Moreover, there may be no ongoing advice to service your constantly evolving needs.

(6) The more money you have, the easier it will be to find a fee-based financial planner, particularly one that charges a "percent of assets" fee. Such planners will find you! While having a lot of money doesn't necessarily mean that your finances are more complex, it does mean you'll be paying more. The most obvious difference between someone who pays a 1 percent fee on $200,000 of assets (or $2,000) and someone who pays a 1 percent fee on $2 million of assets (or $20,000) is that the latter paid ten times more! But was the advice he received ten times more helpful, or complex, or needed? You'll have to be the judge. Just recognize that you'll probably do best to think in terms of flat numbers when you ask yourself how much you would pay for advice on your finances (i.e., "I would pay up to $5,000, and I'm going to negotiate down the percentages with any planner who's fishing for easy money with percentage-based payment plans").

(7) Whatever the fees, ask yourself if you're getting commensurate value. The more you shop around or study up, the better prepared you'll be to answer and reanswer that question.

(8) Those with investable assets below $100,000 will usually have a tough time finding a fee-based planner. Moreover, for those same people who seek only occasional advice, an annual asset-based fee is usually an expensive proposition relative to the payback. An hourly charge makes more sense. If this is you, expect to take a little more time and effort to find a good planner. It's unlikely that one will knock on your door.

(9) Particularly for this last group, we offer a fee-only service called TMF Money Advisor, which provides completely independent financial advice for any money situation, at around two hundred dollars a year (as opposed to a couple hundred an hour). We won't spend lots of space promoting this service, but if you're interested, you can inquire further at Fool.com, or just type "TMF Money Advisor" into the Google.com search engine.

(10) Finally, make sure you connect the dots between how you're paying your financial advisor and what he or she might be recommending. Ideally, these things are disconnected. Ideally, your advisor is simply advising you to find and invest in the best stuff. Try

to avoid the trap that so many fall into, which is to hire a financial advisor from Big Brokerage Firm Inc. who ends up charging both for the advice *and* for selling an entire plan invested primarily in assets bearing Big Brokerage Firm Inc.'s brand, complete with Big Brokerage Firm Inc.'s exorbitant fees. Need we say more?

CONDUCTING THE FINANCIAL-PLANNER INTERVIEW

We've gone over how to select a good financial advisor and how they are paid. Let's talk a bit about the initial interview you should conduct with prospective advisors. We'll assume you've already, to the extent possible, run your own background check (i.e., obtained referrals, asked around). That concluded, most of the questions you'll want to pose to a financial planner fall within four categories.

Here's a Foolish acronym you can use as a mnemonic.

You ready?

FACE!

FACE stands for:

F—Fees: How much will the expert charge? How does he or she get paid?

A—ADV form (or the state-securities-agency equivalent): This document (Uniform Application for Investment Advisor Registration) filed with the Securities and Exchange Commission that discloses educational and business background, compensation, and investment methodology. You want to see it.

C—Credentials: As we mentioned before, there's little regulation in the industry. Still, the lowest charlatans don't have and can't use these designations, so the credentials are at least one indicator of quality. Or, more accurate: The lack of any credentials is most telling.

E—Experience: How long has the financial professional been doing business, and has she done similar work in the past?

Okay, so will you find the perfect planner overnight? Not necessarily, unless you have a really productive day. But so what? This isn't a process you want to hurry. When you need expert advice, you want to be extremely confident that you've found the right person. That kind of confidence is almost always achieved through your own efforts.

FACE!

WHEN TO FIRE
YOUR FINANCIAL PLANNER

You've probably picked up by now that we don't ever think you should relinquish all financial thinking to a third party, particularly if he or she urges or insists that you do so. That's Fire the Planner situation number one.

Another warning sign: Someone in life-insurance sales seeks out your business, offering a free consultation. No, thank you! Trust us on that one. That's Fire the Planner situation number two.

If you are looking to buy simple financial products, such as term-life or automobile insurance, you can more easily and effectively research and purchase them online, either on your own or with the help of a friend. The fees you would pay a financial planner for these services are a waste of money, as he or she should tell you. If not, that's Fire the Planner situation number three.

If you don't have a lot of money, and your finances are not complex, you probably do not need a full-blown, detailed financial plan or historical tax audit in exchange for $2,000 of your meager savings. That's Fire the Planner situation number four, though, really, it's more about hiring, not firing: hiring the right person for the right circumstances. You just want to check in and chat with someone who can add a little expert context to your financial situation, an hour here or there.

There are certainly worse Fire the Planner situations, but those should be pretty obvious. We've highlighted subtler considerations than, say, outright embezzlement.

"Embezzlement" is too harsh a way to end what should be a positive chapter. So let's let slip the dogs, as promised. (Enter a hundred different breeds, "Arf arf arf," with attendant puppy-dog looks.) You see these fellas? They're man's best friend, it is said.

Yeah . . . well? No more!

Good financial advisors will make you far more money! They are better than dogs.

Action Plan

■ Determine whether you need help. There are times in life when a second opinion is especially welcome: dealing with estate issues after the death of a parent; handling complicated stock-option decisions; making sure that your kids, not Uncle Sam, are the major beneficiaries of your estate.

■ Start sleuthing. Ask trusted friends and family for recommendations. Who have they used? Were they happy with the service? How did they find the pro? Would they hire this person again? If you need additional recommendations, ask fellow Fool Community members by visiting http://boards.fool.com (a thirty-day free trial is available).

■ Do your homework. Start your reconnaissance with the folks who were recommended to you. Get some information on the phone and then make appointments with those who look promising. Check out their credentials, too—learn exactly what those initials stand for. You'll find details on many credentials at this Web page: http://iua.americancentury.com/iua/using_advisor/advisor_credentials.jsp.

■ Grill 'em. How often will you meet with your financial planner? What specific services will she provide? What if problems or questions arise? Will you work directly with her, or will your file be handed off to an associate? Has she handled situations like yours before? It's pretty easy to find out the answers to these questions: Just ask.

Chapter Eight

Owning the Right Home

Fare you well, old house! you're naught that can feel or see,
But you seem like a human bein'—a dear old friend to me;
And we never will have a better home, if my opinion stands,
Until we commence a-keepin' house in the house not made with hands.

—WILL CARLETON

OUR "HAVING ENOUGH" section would not be complete—you wouldn't have enough—if we didn't Foolishly examine two more critical topics: owning the right home (this chapter's focus) and the gnarly and troublesome beast that is health care ("Beware the Jabberwock, my son! The jaws that bite, the claws that catch!").

Shall we start with some numbers? Basic stuff. Let's.

The size of the average house in America has grown more than 50 percent in the last thirty years, from about 1,500 square feet to 2,300 square feet. Meanwhile, U.S. population growth, courtesy of contraception and planning, has leveled off. The 2000 census shows that the average family comes to something just short of 3.25 people (don't ask us what 0.25 of a person is—ask the census people). Do the math and you'll recognize that the American family, with the same number of people, is demanding more and more square footage.

What a wonderful development for those who can afford it!

You have the modern kitchen with island stove, the expansive home office, the exercise room, and something that used to be called a living room but these days may resemble a megaplex movie theater. You have the master bedroom with a bed that could pass for the landing platform on an aircraft carrier. You've even refinished the basement, cozy little English tearoom that it now is.

Okay, fine, that might not sound exactly like your house. But if you looked at the American home today through the eyes of a middle-aged couple in 1943, they'd put it much like that. Our living space has gotten bigger. *Much* bigger.

Only problem is, many people can't afford all this space if they seek financial independence in the time they can truly enjoy it. Furthermore, how many truly need *all* that space? If you don't want to part with the home office, beautiful kitchen, luxurious bathrooms, and that theatrical "living room," fine. But what about your children's bedrooms? Once they move out, that space is pretty much empty, unless you plan on inviting your college graduates to live at home. If not, how useful are those rooms to you going forward?

If you plan to depart the world of formal employment sooner rather than later, it's definitely time to rethink your residence. The housing situation for baby boomers leads to some curious contradictions. The average family is overspending, with underfunded retirement plans and extra space in the home. Even if that doesn't perfectly summarize you, it's nevertheless time to ask, once you hit your fiftieth year, "Should I continue owning this place?"

WELL, SHOULD YOU CONTINUE OWNING THAT PLACE?

The following questions provide clues:

Do you feel secure about your retirement savings and the rising cost of health care?

Do you sleep easy, expecting to help your kids through college, to take care of your parents as they prepare for heaven, and to still have enough to last into your nineties?

How important is it to maintain your present living standard through your retirement?

How important are the untouched children's bedrooms?

Could you invest your real estate monies more creatively, more intelligently?

If your answer falls anywhere between "I'm not sure" and "Yeah, my house is too big," we can tell you this: All the demographics (family size, house size, family savings, family debt, projected longevity) suggest that you sit with the majority. Mind you, we have no interest in lining you up and marching you into a life of dime-counting misery on a dusty old couch in something best called a hovel. That was your sophomore year in college. Times have changed. You've come a long way, boomers.

But what about a handsome—*smaller*—jewel box of a home? And what if it led to a simpler life, perhaps just a half mile from a golf course or fishing hole, with the attendant elimination of unnecessary belongings and unused space?

The answer for most baby boomers is to seriously consider a smaller home, a simpler life . . . *and the resulting boost to your compiled and annual savings.* If you're anywhere near the median, you (a) own too much home for your finances, (b) own too much home for your present and future needs, and (c) have way too much stuff in your home (pick a random closet, and you'll shock us if you've used more than half the belongings in there in the last year).

At the same time, we know that most of us don't feel motivated to go through a change of residence. The move, the hideous day of the move. You haven't slept well for six days. You're moving farther away from friends. You're coughing up dust mites from packing all that old stuff. You just got hammered by your spouse for forgetting to pack the attic. Some guy named Sammy drops your antique bureau en route to the moving truck.

Doggone it, why did you ever decide to move?

But wait.

Do you really want to lag behind all those smart baby boomers downshifting into more affordable homes? The market for single-family homes is far more attractive now than it will be during the major housing transitions we'll see over the next fifteen years. Furthermore, the sooner you draw capital from an asset that provides middling long-term returns (real estate) and direct it into an asset that provides excellent long-term returns (the general stock market), the more security you'll earn over the next quarter century.

That's all particularly true given recent history. The extended bear market in equities, alongside the extended bull market in real estate, creates a nice new reverse play for investors: out of real estate into equities. If you want to be financially contrary, you'll have to anticipate (a) the aging population's move into smaller dwellings; (b) the stock market's long-term reversal from bear to bull; and (c) the long-term steadying of the real estate market.

THE NEW WAY OF SEEING

As we've been hinting, the major reasons to move into a smaller home are not all financial, but the financial benefits shine brightly on your plans for retirement. First up, a few years ago Congress gave homeowners a smooch in the form of the Taxpayer Relief Act of 1997. The act allows you to sell your house and protect gains of up to $250,000 ($500,000 per couple) from all taxes. That opens the door on "boutique living," our new term for setting yourself up anew in a more appropriately sized home with far fewer piles of stuff on every table, in every closet, on every bookshelf, in every corner of the attic. Yes, we think baby boomers should be net sellers of large homes and their accompanying mountains of belongings (hello again, eBay).

Imagine selling your house and purchasing a new, smaller one with a minimum down payment on a thirty-year mortgage. Lenders love to carry retiree mortgages because they have a very low default rate. Then you could Foolishly invest the remaining cash (up to $500,000 in gains *tax-free*) at more attractive rates of return. Will that work for you? You'll know only if you run the numbers yourself. Naturally, there are a host of right answers.

For some, it'll be smarter to stay put (your home's the right size; your neighbors are family; the economics of your retirement don't frighten you). For others, it'll make the most sense to sell the family home, buy two itsy-bitsy cottages (winter in Tucson, summer in Coos Bay), and wind up with more cash for your back-end years. For others, it'll be smarter to rent (you've dreamed of mobility and shedding responsibilities and already made a down payment on a Winnebago). Still others will choose to buy a larger home (you've invited your children and theirs to move in with you without consulting us first—what the heck are you thinking?!).

Whether you own or rent, sell or stay put, do recognize that your home is more than a house. The house is just a structure of sticks and bricks, walls and beams. As such, it has monetary value. That value can and should be used when needed. Our task as Fools is to determine if and when that's appropriate. Why? Because we believe you can make a better *home* out of a house that fits your financial profile, the possibly reduced number of occupants, and your changing lifestyle. That may mean getting a place with an exercise room, a home office, and a studio to replace those children's bedrooms. (Hey, you still love your offspring, but this ain't no vacant bed-and-breakfast).

DITCHING YOUR HOUSE: A CASE STUDY

Let's hypothetically illustrate some of the points made above.

Imagine Ozzy and Sharon, two forty-five-year-old boomers living in a house worth $220,000. They bought it for $170,000 five years ago and now have $150,000 of equity in the place.

Let's say that, in order to generate some investable money, they sell the house and move somewhere less expensive. Assume that the proceeds from the sale of their house are $220,000, and they have to pay off the remaining $20,000 that they owed on the house. This leaves them with $200,000. Since they lived in their house long enough and they qualify per other rules, Uncle Sam will allow them up to $500,000 in tax-free capital gains on the sale of their home—$250,000 for each of them. This means their profits are not taxed.

Ozzy and Sharon now have $200,000 in their hot little hands but no roof over their heads. (Okay, they probably should do things in a slightly different order, arranging their new housing first, but we're dealing in the hypothetical, so let's make them wild and impulsive.) They could live under a big umbrella down by the river for the next twenty years and invest the $200,000, but that's not ideal. (Though earning an average of 11 percent a year in an index fund would grow that to $1.6 million in twenty years!)

If they can find a suitable but more modest place, they may do quite well. Let's say they find a charming $160,000 bungalow. They buy it with 20 percent down, or $32,000, plus $3,000 in closing costs—a total of $35,000. So their new mortgage is for $125,000 ($160,000 less $35,000). If they luck out with a good interest rate, such as 7 percent, their monthly payments on a thirty-year fixed mortgage would be just $850, possibly less than they had been paying previously. This alone might save them money each month. If they opt for a fifteen-year fixed-rate mortgage, payments would be a perhaps still manageable $1,150. (Note that other kinds of mortgages are available and might suit their needs better.)

Let's recap where they stand now. They're in a new home, having laid out $35,000 of their $200,000 sale proceeds. That leaves them with $165,000. If they invest this amount in an index fund that earns the market's historical average return of 11 percent over twenty years, it would grow to $1.3 million. (If it grows an average of just 9 percent—always possible, have you checked your stocks lately?—the total would be $925,000.)

What has really happened here? Well, instead of leaving their $150,000 of equity in their house to grow, they've moved it (and a bit more) into the stock market, which has (on average—no guarantees) grown at a faster clip. Your situation will vary a bit. Everyone's will, as there are many parts to this example. Especially if you're wild and impulsive.

The following factors can make big differences in your options.

(1) How much equity you have in your house
(2) What kind of housing market you live in and how much, if anything, your place might be expected to appreciate in the coming decades
(3) Your risk temperament (you might even invest much of your new money in bonds, if you prefer)
(4) Your alternative housing options (can you find less expensive satisfactory housing?)
(5) Your future plans (did you want or need to have your home paid off? were you going to leave a paid-off house to your children in ten years?)

NEW WORLD, NEW POSSIBILITIES

You needn't go out and buy a traditional new home.

Older-age living comes in increasingly more and more flavors.

You can expect some additional wonderful new varieties as well. Communities will spring up near universities and cultural hubs. Second and third homes, apartments, or condominiums are in. The walk-in closet might become a staple. Assisted-living and nursing homes will gain in comfort and care over the next twenty years. The residential options will continuously expand. (Hey, *dude*, the golden days of communes might even return!) Communities will spring up around common interests and philosophies . . . why not a Motley Fool retirement community in Las Cruces, New Mexico? Who knows what else might happen. Heck, time-shares might go from being the favorite pitch of a crooked sales-person to a reasonably attractive option for the mobile.

(Foolish Note: If you're considering a time-share, please, please, please take your time. Run the numbers. Read the prospectus. Laugh at hard-nosed salespeople. Get a listing of all fees. Seek help from your friends and family on the decision. Also, check out the thousands of time-shares that are being resold at a fraction of their original cost on websites like www.vacationresellers.com. Sorry for this extended note, but some of the more destructive sales jobs over the past decade have been done in advocacy of time-shares.)

So many variations of housing are springing up today, to meet those forty and over, that we'd be uneconomical with our words and your time if we spent much more than a few extra thoughts on some of the primary options.

(1) **Staying put.** Nothing newfangled here, but we're going to say it again: This makes sense if you love your neighbors, love the building you live in, can easily afford the place, have well-funded retirement plans, and are willing to do a massive clean-out of old stuff. Even if you're not moving, you should prepare for a move and shrink the inventory in your place.

(2) **Boutique living, aka the smaller home.** We favor this option for many in their forties and fifties today. Remember, you can downsize into a smaller, less expensive home right around the corner if you love your 'hood. If you leave town for a smaller place, please either rent beforehand or take an extended trip to whatever towns you're giving serious consideration.

(3) **Buying a condominium.** A fine option as well. The option of replacing a large family home with two smaller condominiums—

one on the beach, one in the mountains—sounds great to us. (Drop us invites at your leisure.) Just remember to do the following: (a) talk with some of the existing unit owners; (b) calculate the annual cost of condominium insurance; and (c) understand all conditions of the monthly condominium fee.

(4) **Moving to a retirement community.** Some of our younger readers likely gasp in horror at the notion of sliding past giant digitally controlled wrought-iron gates into cookie-cutter retirement communities where everyone presumably looks the same, has backyard bushes full of misfired golf balls, drives half blindly and dangerously, and fights for the last slice of baklava in the corner convenience store. If so, it's time to shed your notions of what such a community can be. Present-day retirement communities are becoming more diverse in age, background, interests, and needs. If you do ultimately lean toward retirement communities, definitely attempt to rent a place first. Get to know the neighbors, the modern conveniences, the personality of the place, and its approach to security.

You get the general point: Put your living situation in the context of your *financial needs* and your *future interests.* Simple statistics together with our own horse sense tell us that this next generation of older Americans presently owns too much home for its needs, alongside too little capital to fund the glory days of its seventh, eighth, and ninth decades on the planet.

Don't delay. Own the right-size dwelling for the decades to come, dear Fool.

Action Plan

■ Stroll around your estate and look it over. Give some serious thought to downsizing or changing your home. Think about whether a change could be advantageous for you financially.

■ If a change seems like it might be worthwhile, don't let yourself get freaked out by the idea. Ease into it by thinking about it for a while. Explore some options. Go to some open houses in the neighborhood where you might relocate. See what kinds of homes are available in the price range you're aiming for. Learn what kinds of prices homes like your current one are fetching. Explore real estate online, perhaps at www.realtor.com, http://realestate.yahoo.com, or http://houseandhome.msn.com.

■ If you're thinking of relocating to a new region, perhaps for a better climate or to be nearer to family, then spend a few weeks there, exploring neighborhoods and the housing market. Get a feel for how you'd like living there.

■ Crunch some numbers to see just how much you can save by moving.

■ Finally, whether a move is or isn't in your near future, down-size your belongings. Sure, you can put it off for another ten or twenty years, but your body will be creaking a bit by then, and the work will be harder. Do it now—get rid of piles of things you never use—and you'll save yourself or your loved ones a lot of trouble in the future.

Chapter Nine

The Right Health Care, the Right Price

And he that will this health deny,
Down among the dead men let him lie.
—ANONYMOUS

 PERHAPS YOU'VE BEEN dreading this chapter from the very start.

We will now untangle the health-care mess while attempting to keep you engaged.

Onward.

When most of us think of health care for retirees, we think Medicare. The majority of working Americans pay in to the program (or are married to someone who does) and anticipate benefits starting at age sixty-five.

Thankfully, the Medicare program covers all health-care costs. Just by paying in, you lock in medical care for the rest of your life. Medicare is rock-solid financially. And if you're anywhere between the ages of forty and sixty, your enrollment will guarantee first-rate medical care for the rest of your life.

Oh, if only.

If only, if only, if only . . .

Unfortunately, the reverse of much of our introduction is true. As today's baby boomers race toward age sixty-five, they will have to worry more about doctor bills than ever before. They'll face the dastardly combination of higher costs and less coverage, even as Medicare struggles with financial stability. That is all bad news.

Let's consider the four primary culprits.

THE BAD NEWS OF HEALTH CARE

CULPRIT #1: MOTHER NATURE

Natural forces conspire against us. Gravity, employment, procreation, and Doritos all take their toll. As you roll into your later years, your body needs more care than it did before. Your lower lumbar region is shouting, "Why should you get to hit golf balls all day while, check it out, *I'm still working?*" Your bladder chimes in, "Yeah, hey," chug-chug-chug, "I'm working harder than ever over here." Eventually, most of your body parts will—like bad employee relations—join the chorus, leading to a general strike.

You *are* the sum of your parts, and those parts will need more attention as you age. That attention isn't free. According to the Health and Human Services Department, older Americans paid an average $3,493 in out-of-pocket health-care expenses. And that was before the cost of health care began its three-year streak of double-digit increases starting in 2001.

The costs are only heading higher, at rates that top inflation. You will, by virtue of the massive and growing demand for health care by the 75 million people heading toward retirement, pay more and get less care over the next two decades. It's simple supply and demand.

CULPRIT #2: UNCLE SAM

We've all heard that the Social Security program is in trouble. But our government's Medicare program (partly funded, in case you need the reminder, by the FICA taxes taken out of your paycheck) is in as much or more danger. Program spending is expected to increase from 2.5 percent of America's gross domestic product (GDP) in 2002 to 5.3 percent of GDP in 2035. But the revenues that pay those costs (i.e., taxes) will rise to just 3.7 percent of GDP in 2030.

In other words, Houston, we have a shortfall.

How can we bridge it? So far, no one in Washington has effected a solution. The 2003 report of the trustees who run the Social Security and Medicare trust funds suggests that the solution must come from either or some combination of: an 83 percent increase in payroll taxes or a 42 percent cut in benefits. Hey, let's repeat that for effect: Medicare solvency will depend on either an 83 percent increase in your payroll taxes, a 42 percent cut in your health-care benefits, or some combination of the two.

That won't come easy.

You can bet that the Medicare of the future, of *your* future, will not be able to cover as many costs as it does today. You will have to pay a greater portion of health-care bills than a seventy-five-year-old does today, and probabilities suggest you'll get less attention and care for your dollars. Yep, we're repeating that point and will continue to!

CULPRIT #3: LAWYERS, DOCTORS, DRUG COMPANIES, AND INSURANCE COMPANIES

For the past several years, overall inflation has been tame. However, certain expense categories have bucked the trend, rising at rates that remind people of the inflationary 1970s. Among the most egregious of these categories is health care. A host of factors—unbridled drug costs, expensive malpractice insurance, rising labor costs for health-care workers, and inefficient insurance companies—have colluded to drive costs ever higher.

Let's consider some numbers.

Total health-care spending per person rose 310 percent from 1977 to 1996, compared to a 159 percent climb in inflation, according to AARP. And that does *not* include the cost of nursing-home care. Over that same period, the cost of prescription drugs as a percentage of health-care spending increased from 6 percent to 15 percent. In other words, drug costs have raced wildly higher over the past few decades.

Unfortunately, these trends are only worsening.

According to the Agency for Healthcare Research and Quality (AHRQ), total expenditures on health care rose from $548 billion in 1996 to $628 billion in 2000. As for prescription drugs, the Kaiser Family Foundation says total spending increased 44 percent from 2000 to 2003.

Culprit #4: You

Yes, you, too, are to blame. You demand the best medical care, and you've shown the willingness to pay for it, which isn't a recipe for low prices. You also may not have been taking the best care of yourself. May we suggest natural and organic foods, a robust daily walk, and a relentless focus on doing what you love? Taking care of yourself becomes a real priority in a world where you will get less health care at higher costs (oh, but we've already painted that picture).

Thankfully, many of the 75 million Americans nearing a part- or full-time departure from the workforce *are* changing their habits. Medical technology is also improving, and the result should be higher life expectancies breaking all records. So if you're fifty years old, expect to live another thirty-five years. If you make it to sixty-five, expect to live another twenty-five. That means get ready to pay for health care longer than any generation in the history of our glorious, imperfect species. It'll take a lot of maintenance to keep your body running into your nineties.

Medicare won't be able to keep up with all the costs. Also get ready to spend a lot of money on tune-ups, overhauls, and body work. Your health is, in the end, *your responsibility*, not your doctor's or the government's. That probably goes without saying, but no one feels the consequences of your lifestyle decisions, for better or for worse, as acutely as you do. No one cares, it turns out, as much about your physical and financial health as you and your family do.

The Enough-Bad-News-for-Now Bottom Line

The bottom line is this: As you project what your living expenses will be in retirement, you'll have to allocate more and more cash to corporeal upkeep.

THE GOOD NEWS: WHAT MEDICARE *WILL* COVER

Medicare won't cover everything, but it will cover a wide range of medical expenses (Botox fans, don't get your hopes up). Let's start with an overview of the Medicare program.

And let us prepare you: These next few pages won't compare well to the work of Dickens, Frost, Austen, or Shakespeare. But fight through with us, because our aim is both beneficial and important—to help you make better decisions about your healthcare spending.

Play the trumpets, bandleader!

Here comes our overview of Medicare!

Medicare is a form of medical insurance funded partially by the government and partially by you. It has two parts. Part A covers hospitalization. Anyone who is sixty-five years old and has paid FICA taxes during their working career (or has been married to someone who did) will be eligible for Part A hospitalization at no additional cost. Bravo.

Part B covers physician services, preventive care, some durable medical devices, and various other medical services (though not regular checkups). Part B has a monthly premium that changes each year. For 2003 the Part B monthly premium was $58.70 per person, or $704.40 for the year.

You become automatically enrolled in Part B if you receive Social Security benefits, and the premiums are taken out of your Social Security check. You should receive a Medicare card about three months before you turn sixty-five. If you don't want Part B, you don't have to pony up the cash. However, it's a good deal for most people. Further, for every twelve months after you turn sixty-five that you *don't* enroll in Part B, the premium permanently increases 10 percent per year that you've delayed enrollment. (That won't happen if you didn't sign up because you're still working and covered under your employer's health plan. In fact, under some circumstances, Medicare will supplement the employer-provided insurance for eligible workers and their spouses.)

Clearly, don't delay.

Even if you don't receive Social Security benefits, you can still sign up for Medicare Part B. You can enroll as early as three months before you turn sixty-five. If you wait longer than three months after you turn sixty-five, you may be subject to the aforementioned 10 percent premium increase. Thus, it pays to know not only what Medicare covers but also when you can (and must) enroll.

Again, we think Medicare's Part B is a must.

GETTING MORE INFORMATION ON HOW MEDICARE WORKS

We could conduct an entire seminar on Medicare. What a blast! But we don't need to, because the Medicare website (www. medicare.gov) offers plenty of information. For a comprehensive description of the program, visit the "Publications" page. (In particular, check out "Medicare and You.") AARP also provides helpful guidance, especially through its excellent "Medicare Basics" publication.

Hey, we know that spending a few hours reading about Medicare isn't at the top of your "What I Love to Do" list. But if you spend the time now, you won't face the nightmares that may come to haunt the unprepared. We are headed for some troubled health-care waters over the next few decades. Learn about your options now, and you'll know how to navigate the storms.

As we've already pointed out, Medicare doesn't cover all costs. All manner of deductibles and copayments are involved. Also, many important medical necessities—such as prescription drugs and dental care—aren't covered by the basic Medicare program. Even if you require a service that *is* covered, be prepared to shell out for deductibles, copayments, and complete coverage after your benefits have been exhausted.

Time for a quick example.

Let's walk through in-patient hospital care, which is covered by Part A (amounts listed below are as of 2003).

- Within the benefit period (ninety days), you're responsible for paying in the first $840.
- This deductible paid, Medicare will cover any remaining costs (due to extended stay) for those first sixty days.
- For days sixty-one to ninety, should you need them, you're responsible for $210 a day.
- For days ninety-one to one hundred fifty of a hospital stay, you'll have to dip into your sixty lifetime reserve days, which can be used just once. At this point, you'll be responsible for costs up to $420 per day.

    From day one hundred fifty-one and onward, you're on your own.

Even though a service or procedure is "covered" by Medicare, that does *not* mean you can carelessly, endlessly bask in the warm glow of the doctor's light without worrying about who's footing the bill. Before you leave full-time employment and the health plan that usually goes with it, you need to know what will be covered via Medicare and how much you'll be expected to contribute.

Now, did you know there are multiple Medicare plans?

You betcha—just to add in a bit more complication, eh?

Let's look at some of the choices.

YOUR CHOICE OF MEDICARE HEALTH PLANS

Depending on where you live, you could have a choice about which Medicare program to enroll in. They include:

■ **The Original Medicare Plan (aka fee-for-service).** This is the basic plan available throughout the country. It offers the most choice in terms of who provides your medical services, but it also results in the most out-of-pocket expenses. And the plan does not offer any extra benefits. Enrollees in this plan need Medigap insurance (see facing page).

■ **The Medicare + Choice Plan.** This plan actually provides a choice of two. The first is a Medicare managed-care plan, which is just like a health-maintenance organization (HMO). In other words, you have to use the in-plan services and specialists. However, it usually results in extra benefits such as prescription drugs and dental care and lower out-of-pocket expenses. The other type of Medicare + Choice plan is the Private Fee-for-Service plan, which is a blend of the two plans.

To help you decide which plan is right for you, the Medicare website offers a Medicare Health Plan Compare tool that tells you what's available in your area. It can be found at http://www.medicare.gov/mphcompare/home.asp.

MEDIGAP INSURANCE

If you enroll in the original Medicare plan, there will be some . . . well . . . gaps in your coverage. In fact, the basic fee-for-service plan covers about half the costs of health care. For many Americans, the slack is picked up by their former employers, who offer health insurance as a retirement benefit. However, the number of businesses offering this benefit is shrinking. A Kaiser Family Foundation survey found that the percentage of companies with two hundred or more workers that offer retiree health benefits has dropped from 66 percent in 1988 to 34 percent in 2002. The services from those that still do are also shrinking. With 50 percent of your health care covered by the basic Original Care plan, and with employers reducing their investment in retiree benefits, more of the burden falls to you.

How do you bridge the gap?

Enter stage left, Medigap supplemental insurance, which is offered by private companies but highly regulated by the states. In all states (except Massachusetts, Minnesota, and Wisconsin), Medigap must be included among ten different policies (labeled A to J) that in effect provide standardized coverage from state to state.

As policy coverage proceeds from A to J, the coverage gets better and the premiums get higher. The average annual Medigap premium in 2003 was $1,056.54 for policy A, $1,626.68 for policy F, and $2,733.73 for policy J, according to Weiss Ratings (which, by the way, provides a report on supplemental insurance options based on a person's age, gender, and zip code—find out more at www.weissratings.com).

The trick is to match the coverage with your needs.

How do you determine your needs?

Get a policy that will cover your health problems and those that run in your family, and try to hold off on excess coverage. Taking stock of where you are, mentally and physically, and reviewing your family health history are critical steps. Once you've gone through your own checkup, it's time to shop around. Even though the coverage of the different Medigap policies is standard, the cost of the policies isn't. Different insurance companies price various health conditions differently, so it will pay to shop around.

If you have any questions about Medicare and Medigap, or would like to order publications, call 1-800-MEDICARE. If you and/or your spouse are still working after age sixty-five and receiving health benefits, you may not need a Medigap policy.

Finally, enrolling in Medicare Part B opens a six-month window during which you can sign up for Medigap and not be turned down for preexisting health conditions. That is critical. So don't dawdle when choosing your supplemental insurance!

BACK TO THE BAD NEWS: WHAT MEDICARE AND MEDIGAP WON'T COVER

Yes, more bad news.

Even if you have Medigap insurance or coverage from a former employer, you will still be responsible for hundreds to thousands of dollars of copayments and deductibles. Be prepared for more out-of-pocket expenses.

One of the bigger expenses retirees face is prescription drugs. Previously, Medicare was no help here, and only three of the ten Medigap policies provided coverage on pharmaceuticals. That changed with the Medicare prescription drug plan signed into law in 2003 . . . sorta. The new plan should save beneficiaries an average $1,300 a year. Folks who sign up with the plan will get 75 percent of their drug costs covered, up to $2,250. Then, coverage stops until the beneficiary has spent another $2,850 out of pocket. After that, the plan will cover 95 percent of costs. There are also extra benefits for lower-income recipients. In other words, you'll still be responsible for plenty of the cost. But it will offer relief to those who have catastrophic drug bills.

LONG-TERM CARE INSURANCE

Something else Medicare generally won't cover is long-term care.

Long-term care encompasses everything from getting help around the house to a lengthy stay in a nursing home. In general, long-term care is the help needed to perform one or more of what modern-day jargon calls "Activities of Daily Living." The National Center for Health Statistics, along with many insurance companies, includes among these activities bathing, dressing, eating, transferring in or out of a bed or chair, and using the toilet. The center uses a second designation, "Instrumental Activities of Daily Living," to account for activities essential to leading an independent life in the community, such as managing money, doing housework, taking medications, shopping, preparing meals, and using the telephone.

Taking a broad view of long-term care, a report published by AARP entitled "Mid-Life and Older Americans with Disabilities" states that in 1994 some 9.5 million Americans aged fifty or older received help for one or more of the Activities (Instrumental or otherwise) listed above. Of those, 1.6 million received help for two or more of the five basic Activities of Daily Living. The one needed most was bathing, followed by dressing, transferring, toileting, and eating, in that order. The Instrumental Activity needed most (sorry about the jargon—it's theirs, not ours) was heavy housework, followed by shopping, light housework, meal preparation, managing money, and using the telephone.

You may not be prepared to think about needing help bathing, but you should begin preparing financially for it. Medicare covers a *very* limited amount of long-term care, and only after the patient meets certain criteria. Medicaid—the health program for the very poor—will pay for long-term care, but not until most assets and income have been exhausted. That's not a situation we want any of our readers to face.

A key takeaway is that increased longevity means an increased chance of needing help in the twilight years. Never to miss a trend, the insurance industry came up with insurance that will help cover the costs of long-term care, and business is booming.

Long-term care insurance policies come in many forms, but all have one thing in common: They ain't cheap. According to research organization LIMRA, the average annual premium on a long-term care policy in 2000 was $1,607, but many policies can cost several thousand dollars more.

Why so expensive?

Because the likelihood you'll need the benefit is high. And the covered service (e.g., nursing-home care), at an average annual cost of well over $60,000, is expensive.

So these policies are expensive. They also happen to be pretty complicated, with loads of features and policy riders to consider. A good deal of self-education is in order, as is a hefty dose of comparison shopping. There's no such thing as a standard long-term care policy, and no such thing as a standard price.

Do you need long-term care insurance?

We've encountered one solid insurance agent who puts it bluntly: "*Get* long-term care insurance, *or* accept the possibility that your children will one day have to change your diapers." Cheery stuff (we chose not to name the fellow). That's one way to look at it. Here, we'll offer up six objective considerations for determining if you should buy long-term care insurance.

(1) The number one source of long-term care is family. Surveys indicate that most elderly Americans would prefer to receive care in their own home from people they know. Members of close-knit families (both emotionally and geographically) naturally find comfort in their children and other relatives. But don't assume you'll receive a high level of family care. Maybe it's time for a family meeting to openly discuss the available options. Realize that even when you're surrounded by willing family members, situations may arise where they're simply unable to care for you.

(2) Most experts recommend that people start researching long-term care insurance once they're in their fifties. Generally speaking, we think *the age of sixty is the right time* to begin a long-term care policy. From that point, for every five years you wait to buy a policy, you can expect to pay 30 to 50 percent more in premiums, as well as run the risk of not being insurable due to declining health. (In fact, one in four applicants for this insurance is turned down.) That said, those who start buying such a policy before their late fifties are buying too early, paying more in premiums than is necessary.

(3) People with sizable savings—well over $1 million in cash and investments—have enough money to pay for long-term care without going broke. The only reason these folks would need long-term care insurance is to protect their estates from a lengthy stay in a nursing home.

(4) Anyone who is behind in retirement savings should max out an IRA or 401(k) before worrying about long-term care insurance.

(5) Americans with assets below $100,000 might prefer to cast their lot with the Medicaid program (see sidebar).

MEDICAID AND LONG-TERM CARE

One of the biggest funding sources for long-term care is Medicaid, the government-funded health program for low-income citizens. Given the high costs of nursing homes and other services, it doesn't take long for someone to run out of assets. That's precisely what must happen before you can become eligible for Medicaid: You have to lose just about everything. Once that happens, most of the costs are covered.

We don't think you want to get there, though.

Mistakenly, some Americans choose not to purchase long-term care insurance because they feel certain Uncle Sam will eventually come to the rescue. But if you rely on the Medicaid program to provide your long-term care, you lose most of the control over where and how you will receive it. Most assisted-living facilities do not accept Medicaid. Most nursing homes do, but there's often a waiting list. Availability may dictate that you end up in a home farther from family, or one that doesn't provide top-notch care, with no assets to improve your lot.

Better to prepare financially and purchase long-term care insurance than to count on the guv'ment to provide for you.

---

(6) One of the greatest benefits of insurance is peace of mind. Anyone worried about affording quality long-term care should look into getting insurance.

What to Look for in a Long-term Care Policy

Okay, let's talk about what you'll want in your long-term care policy.

Start off by looking for insurance companies that are highly rated by Standard & Poor's and Moody's. Since you might pay premiums on the policy for decades, you want to choose a company that'll be around when it's time to cash in.

Consider the following features.

- **The daily benefit.** Policies will pay a certain amount for every day the beneficiary receives care. The average cost of nursing-home care is approximately $175 per day. However, the price of care varies widely from state to state; you'll definitely want to find out how much it costs in your area. You won't need a policy that covers *all* the costs, since you should still be receiving income from sources such as Social Security and a pension. So look for a policy that covers 80 to 90 percent of the costs in your area, which will result in lower policy premiums.

- **Inflation protection.** Just as medical costs are rising rapidly, so is the price of long-term care. At a yearly price hike of 6 percent—disappointingly high, though a much smaller amount than what we've seen in medical costs—the purchasing power of a $150 daily benefit will be halved in twelve years. A policy with a benefit that rises alongside inflation will cost extra but may be worth it, especially if the beneficiary is young. Consider inflation protection.

- **The elimination period.** The longer the period between when you need care and when your policy pays off (known as the "elimination period"), the lower your premiums should be. Keep in mind that insurance is meant to protect against catastrophic loss, not every little expense. Therefore, look for policies with a thirty- or sixty-day elimination period. Then tuck away the money you save on premiums to spend on those first two months, if needed.

- **Benefit period.** A 1994 Public Policy Institute report stated that the chances of a given American winding up in a nursing home are roughly 52 percent for women and 33 percent for men. The duration of stay for three out of four residents is under a year. Take these findings into account when choosing a benefit period. The same report stated that for Americans sixty-five and older, the average length of stay has been 2.3 years (shorter and shorter, the older the entrant). If you want to be conservative, project a benefit period of three to five years.

- **Home care.** Look for policies that will cover home visits by medical professionals or staff who can assist with the activities of daily living. Some policies either won't cover these services or will pay only a portion of a policy's stated benefit. You definitely want a policy that will pay the same benefit for care you receive in your home as for care in a nursing home.

As you shop around, ask about any discounts the companies offer. Begin searching for deals as early as possible (like tomorrow). You might be able to get a discount if you and your spouse buy policies from the same company. You could perhaps get a group of family members or friends and negotiate a volume discount. (Furthermore, check to see if your employer offers long-term insurance on a group basis.) A lower premium is your aim. Veterans and federal employees should look into the Federal Long Term Care Insurance Program.

One final thought: If you have elderly parents who may need assistance in the coming years, consider their future needs as well. Weigh your potential long-term costs against the cost of long-term care insurance. Enrolling them might be the best gift you ever gave—and among your own better investments, too.

TEN WAYS TO CUT HEALTH-CARE COSTS BEFORE YOU RETIRE

Without further ado, the ten ways to cut health-care costs before you retire:

(1) **Coordinate.** Dual-income couples should coordinate insurance benefits. It might make sense to opt out of one plan and choose the family option on another. On the other hand, maintaining coverage with two providers can make sense if the two complement each other.

(2) **Get a flexible spending account.** This allows you to use pretax money to pay for medical costs not covered by a health plan, such as deductibles, copayments, even eyeglasses. It could shave a few hundred dollars off your tax bill, depending on your medical expenses and tax bracket. Flexible spending accounts are offered by employers as benefits, so ask the good people in your human

resources department for details. If you're self-employed, look into a medical savings account (MSA), which serves a similar function but can be used to supplement retirement savings as well.

(3) **Choose the right health plan.** Most employees have a choice of health plan. The options can range from cheap, without much flexibility (like HMOs), to more expensive plans with more choices (like a preferred provider organization, or PPO). Unless you are significantly benefiting from more choices, opt for the HMO.

(4) **Work with Uncle Sam.** If you incur extraordinary medical expenses in one year, you can deduct from your taxable income the medical costs that exceed 7.5 percent of your adjusted gross income. This can include insurance premiums and a host of other medical-related expenses.

(5) **Freeload!** Take advantage of the free or discounted services offered by your health plan. Many providers will subsidize flu shots, gym memberships, nutrition classes, and other preventive care.

(6) **Check your bills.** According to a *Consumer Reports* survey, 5 percent of patients found serious errors in their hospital bills. Those who paid $2,000 or more out of pocket were twice as likely to find billing boo-boos. The most common blunders include "up-coding" (charging patients for more costly procedures); incorrect basic charges as a result of keystroke errors or canceled work; charging for individual tests that should have been combined (called "unbundled charges"); and overcharging for operating room time, which is calculated by the hour. Nasty stuff. Keep your eyes open. Please, please, look carefully through your bill to verify all charges.

(7) **Raise your copayment or deductible.** If you are a healthy person who doesn't require much medical help, lower your premiums by raising your potential out-of-pocket expenses. (But make sure you have an emergency fund at the ready.)

(8) **Get healthy.** Being healthy is not only good for you, but it will keep your insurance costs down. Small investments in your physical, mental, emotional, and spiritual health today will reap enormous rewards down the line.

(9) **Get rid of insurance you don't need.** Unless you or others will be relying on postretirement income (which sounds like an

oxymoron, but you know what we mean), you don't need life insurance.

(10) **Choose the right supplemental insurance.** Generally, Medicare recipients with Medigap insurance pay the most out-of-pocket expenses, followed by those with employer-sponsored coverage. But even though Medicare + Choice can be cheaper at first glance, it may not offer the flexibility you need; and it's not available throughout the country. Determine what medical care you regularly use and anticipate using (to the extent that's possible), and choose the coverage most conducive to your condition.

MEDICAL INSURANCE FOR YOUNGER RETIREES

If you're younger than sixty-five when you retire, what should you do for insurance? It depends on your situation. We'll provide some general answers, but it's definitely an area you'll have to check out for yourself and tailor to your individual needs.

Go with the group, if possible. While working, you'll typically enjoy medical and health-insurance coverage through a group policy from your employer. Many employers will allow you to carry that coverage into retirement; some will even pay part or all of the cost. Most won't. That means you may have to pay the entire premium, something few of us do while working. Is the cost worth it? In general, the answer is an emphatic yes. A group policy is almost always far cheaper than an individual policy providing the same coverage. For those who retire prior to Medicare eligibility at age sixty-five, a group policy is probably the best route if your employer allows you to keep that coverage when you leave your job.

Your short-term option. What if your employer is one of the many who will not let you continue your group medical insurance after you leave the job? The government has given you some breathing room by mandating your right to remain insured under your employer's policy for up to eighteen months, at your own expense. (In certain instances, spouses and dependents may continue coverage for up to thirty-six months.) Called COBRA (ophidian shorthand for the Consolidated Omnibus Budget Reconciliation Act of 1985), the law provides for continued coverage when you leave your job for reasons other than gross misconduct.

Be aware that the cost of this coverage can be in the hundreds of dollars a month for both families and single persons. And your employer will probably charge you an extra 2 percent for administrative expenses. Therefore, verify the arrangement with your employer prior to leaving the job.

Keep covered. When your COBRA coverage ends, in the absence of Medicare, your only option is an individual or family policy. If you leave your job prior to age sixty-five, you'll almost certainly pay far more for such coverage than you did while working. How much more will depend on your state of residence and the type of coverage selected. Therefore, the earlier you start the research, the easier it will be to incorporate this cost into your financial plans.

MISCELLANEOUS HEALTH-RELATED FACTS AND THOUGHTS

- A study conducted by the employee-benefits consulting firm Watson Wyatt Worldwide found that large employers who typically pay over half of each retiree's medical expenses will be paying under 10 percent by the year 2031. Some have already begun cutting back. A fifth have eliminated retiree health coverage for new hires, and 17 percent will require new hires to pay the full premium for coverage.
- If you retire before you're eligible for Medicare, and your spouse still works, get on his or her plan.
- Including premiums paid, Medicare beneficiaries paid an estimated $2,580 on health care in 2000 (excluding long-term care).
- The premiums for Medigap have increased dramatically over the past several years, but the biggest jumps have been in policies H, I, and J; and those are the only three that will pay part of the costs of prescription drugs. According to Weiss Ratings, these policies have increased on average over 40 percent since 1998.

CHOOSING A NURSING HOME

The final stop on our tour of retirement health care is here, at the local nursing home. Choosing a nursing home for a relative is rarely pleasant. Fortunately, it has gotten easier to compare the different options. The results of a government survey of the nation's 17,000 nursing homes is now available on the Medicare website, at http://www.medicare.gov/nhcompare/home.asp. Consumers can see how a facility was rated in ten categories, including percentage of patients with pain, delirium, and bedsores.

All of this information is based on data that nursing homes must report in order to receive Medicare funds. Also included are the results of annual inspections and complaint investigations. Facilities looking to improve their scores can get advice from the quality-improvement organizations under contract with Medicare.

High-quality nursing-home care doesn't come cheap. A year's stay can cost as little as $35,000, up to as much as $150,000. For those unable to afford such steep prices, Medicaid steps in—after most of the person's assets have been depleted.

It should be obvious that this entire chapter is dedicated to helping you and your loved ones avoid ever having to use Medicaid. Most of the topics reward you for getting to know them better, based on what is most relevant to you. What's the reward? Lower fees. Better care. Fewer surprises. Better family relations. The list could go on.

Let us close this search for your best health care by making what is perhaps the simplest, strongest statement intended to be of benefit to the greatest number of readers:

As you reach age sixty, please consider long-term care insurance as a safety net from here until the hereafter.

Action Plan

- Make sure that health-care costs are factored into your long-range financial plans and budget.
- Learn all about Medicare so you know what to expect and

how to take full advantage of the program. Understand that there are certain steps you need to take and decisions to make at certain times. Click over to www.medicare.gov and read up at www.aarp.org/healthcoverage/, too. Offline, try this book: *Consumer Reports Complete Guide to Health Services for Seniors: What Your Family Needs to Know About Finding and Financing, Medicare, Assisted Living, Nursing Homes, Home Care, Adult Day Care.*

◙ Look into long-term care insurance, starting typically in your late fifties or early sixties. You might even look into helping your parents get it. Consider reading Marilee Driscoll's *The Complete Idiot's Guide to Long-Term Care Planning* and/or *J. K. Lasser's Choosing the Right Long-Term Care Insurance* by Ben Lipson.

◙ If health-care costs and the state of coverage in the United States have you confounded, worried, alarmed, or feeling strongly in any way, consider contacting your representatives in Washington to let them know of your concerns. You can do so very easily online, at www.congress.org.

Section Conclusion

So concludes our section on Having Enough.

Let's keep it short and sweet and get to Having More Than Enough as quickly as possible.

Before heading in, though, let's review our early goals. This first section's aim has been to help you analyze how much you'll need in savings, at what rate you'll need those savings to grow, and how your money should be invested. We opened by asking a question near and dear to our hearts ("Why Retire?") and finally closed with what may be the most perplexing and money-consuming topic of all: funding your health care. In between, we asked: "Should you sell your house to help out?" And we addressed finding advisory help where needed.

Each of these items forms a critical part of Having Enough to retire and retire well. But having enough isn't necessarily enough for every reader of this book. Nosirree. We expect that many will desire *more than enough*—or, even if you don't desire it, you'd be interested in learning more. So let's talk about Having More Than Enough. Get ready to get above average.

PART III

HAVING MORE
THAN ENOUGH

Chapter Ten

Social Insecurity

*Make it your ambition to lead a quiet life, to mind your own business
and to work with your hands, just as we told you, so that your daily life
may win the respect of outsiders and so that you will not be dependent
on anybody.*

—I Thessalonians 4:11–12

 "A Brief History of Social Security," a pamphlet issued in August 2000 marking Social Security's sixty-fifth anniversary, begins with this succinct opening line: "Social Security works because it speaks to a universal human need."

Speak it has, in the trillions of dollars, but how sustainably so is debatable. We doubt we're causing the scales to fall from your eyes, dear reader, when we point out that for over sixty years, Social Security has been a tax levied on Jane to pay John immediately, within any given calendar year. John is older than Jane, and over the course of his life, he was led to believe that he was "building up retirement" by paying Social Security into a "lockbox" that was being "invested" and then paid back to him in the latter part of his life.

Yet there never was any lockbox; the money paid each year in Social Security taxes has been transferred right away to those "owed" their "benefits." It's a pay-as-you-go system. Economists like Henry Hazlitt were accurately foretelling its eventual doom decades ago. However, most Americans have historically trusted the arrangement; few listened much to economist gadflies. Well, and it was the law to pay those taxes.

Today the system is not quite broken. Yet. But it is doomed. Every day the numbers of those retiring and living longer inflate relative to those entering or remaining in the workplace. The urgency for a solution only grows with time, but our government's built-in "get me elected next term" myopia has continued to delay solutions. As many recent calls as there have been to fix or reform Social Security, very few were offered in the spirit of a proposed solution, or taken seriously by our federal government.

We find ourselves with a "retirement program" that faces an eventual crisis on a massive scale. All of which explains why this chapter on what you can expect from Social Security takes the title it does: As solid as it may look, the system is inherently unstable.

Our goal in the few pages ahead is not to reform the system. Perhaps you can write that book—we look forward to reading it! No, our aim here is to help you build your retirement plan. That means helping you answer questions like:

How much Social Security will I be getting?

What additional considerations should I be aware of, like whether or not to begin taking early reduced payments or later full payments?

What changes to the system are likely, and by when?

If they ever existed, the days of relying on Social Security to fund your retirement are gone. Despite the recent period of almost historically low inflation, living costs have continued to accelerate higher than the supposed "returns" that Social Security funds have been obtaining as they were "invested" (okay, we'll try to lay off the sarcastic quotation marks). According to the Social Security Administration, for the year 2002 the average single retiree received $874 in monthly Social Security benefits; the average retired couple received $1,454.

Therefore, no retirement plan should be predicated on Social Security payments. They'll keep coming in their present form for a decade longer and will supplement the retirement of many Americans over that period. But anyone below the age of fifty-five should be thinking very seriously about how the world might change, and how one's plans to retire within it may need to reflect those alterations. We'll provide our guesses at the end of the chapter.

But first, why is this chapter presented in our "Having More Than Enough" section? Why isn't this foundation stone of financial Americana part of just "Having Enough"? Because we think it's both most helpful and most foresighted to treat any Social Security payments you get in the future as *perks*.

WHY WAS SOCIAL SECURITY STARTED?

The Social Security Act was passed in 1935, when life expectancy averaged just under sixty. Congress set the benefits payout for age sixty-five. The idea, as you can see, was that only about half the Americans who paid in would be around to collect those benefits. When you think about it, that's the whole premise of insurance: We all pay in, but only a minority claims the benefits. Social Security was formulated as an insurance plan. As one observer put it, "It is a Depression-era program designed to keep older people out of the poorhouse." It was never designed to become a national pension. Which is the way many people view it today.

That's not surprising. Since all of us have been continuously taxed for years or decades, many of us have come to view it—not unreasonably so—as a form of pension or entitlement. Because, darn it, "I contributed!"

But that was not the original purpose, and likewise, we doubt that'll be the final result.

FOR FURTHER THINKING

George Foreman on why he went broke:

David: George, you said that you came back to boxing because you were broke. We have to think that during that initial boxing career, you made quite a bit of money. What happened to that money along the way?

George Foreman: Well, you have heard of fast women and slow horses? I just had no idea about life, that you needed to save money and look for the future. Even though I boxed for ten years, I thought the money would continue to come every day, and I just spent. I had no idea that one day you would be a middle-aged man and you are going to need money. But you don't want money, I thought. That was the end of it.

HOW MUCH DOES ONE HAVE TO EARN TO CLAIM SOCIAL SECURITY PAYMENTS?

To become eligible for "retirement benefits," as the Social Security Administration calls its payouts (see the final section of this chapter for perspective on that), one has to earn forty "credits." One can earn a maximum of four credits per year, so this is like saying, "You need to have worked for ten years."

What does it take to earn a credit these days? Probably less than you think. At present 2003 rates, one credit is awarded per every $890 of job earnings (working for someone else or self-employed). Somebody who pulls down $3,560 per year in wage earnings in 2003 gets all four annual credits toward that forty needed to become eligible for Social Security. Anyone who does not have those forty credits is not eligible for his or her own Social Security. (You can share in your spouse's, of course.)

If you've traditionally been a stay-at-home mom with a husband who is nearing retirement age and you're both worried you won't have enough, consider this: By working part or full time yourself, you qualify for your own additional Social Security; and any past credits you have through part-time jobs or before you were married still count. Earning $3,560 in the next year may require some adjustments to your lifestyle, but doing so will earn you the maximum four annual credits toward the eventual qualifying forty.

HOW MUCH SOCIAL SECURITY WILL YOU GET?

Social Security income is calculated based on a formula that takes into account the thirty-five years in which you or your spouse earned the most (your "average monthly indexed earnings"), as well as the overall change in average wages since the year you started earning wages. The magic number that pops out—which can't be easily formulated or provided in some catchall form to every reader here—is called your "primary insurance amount" (see, they're calling it insurance!).

You can visit the Social Security website at www.ssa.gov and read a wealth of additional information on the subject. You can even have the Social Security Administration send you a document detailing what you can expect to be paid, based on the information they've gathered about you. (We did this—what the heck—it took about four weeks to show up.) What you'll discover if you're over fifty is that the numbers will play out very similarly to those provided earlier. That is, if you were getting Social Security in 2003, you could count on about $11,000 a year if you were single, or $18,000 a year if you were married. With each passing year, add in 1 to 2 percent to arrive at some ballpark numbers.

This will work as long as the system remains status quo. Unfortunately, the pay-as-you-go scheme is forecast to no longer work by the year 2016. That's when the Social Security Administration is projected to collect less in receipts than it will need to pay out in promises. That should necessitate some changes between today and 2016 A.D.; we'll update this book by then! For now the assumptions above are the most likely.

SHOULD YOU TAKE PAYMENTS AT SIXTY-TWO OR SIXTY-FIVE?

Full Social Security payouts begin at age sixty-five for those born in 1937 or earlier. That age ratchets up in bimonthly increments to sixty-six for those born from 1943 to 1954, and up to sixty-seven for those (like your embattled authors, who will never see one thin dime from this arrangement) born in 1960 or later.

That's for *full* payouts.

As the section headline suggests, you can receive Social Security starting with the first full month that you are sixty-two. However, think about it this way: The *total* gross dollars you will be paid averages the same whether you start taking the money at sixty-five or sixty-two. Thus, if you begin taking Social Security before the age of sixty-five, you'll permanently receive less in monthly payouts over the rest of your life. As a general rule, early payouts mean more payouts but in smaller amounts, to account for the longer period over which you'll receive them.

It is neither always right nor always wrong to take reduced payments by starting early, or to take full benefits by starting late. Here are some contrasting examples. If you knew ahead of time that you were going to die when you were sixty-four, you'd obviously take the payments starting in the very first month. On the other hand, if you are still fit and working at sixty-two for a higher salary than you averaged over the course of your life, you probably neither need the Social Security money at that point nor benefit by taking it early. In that case, keep working and get the fullest, biggest amount you can, beginning at your full retirement age.

The SSA has a helpful table to give you a sense of what percentage your annual payments will be reduced, assuming you take that first payout the first month you can (age sixty-two). Keep in mind that depending on your date of birth, the age at which you get full benefits varies from sixty-five to sixty-seven. The following table shows how the numbers look:

For instance, if you are fifty-four years old in 2003, you were born in 1949 and have a full retirement age of sixty-six. If you take your earliest payout at age sixty-two, you'll be doing so four years—or forty-eight months—ahead of schedule. Because of that, this table shows that your permanent annual payments will come to 25 percent less each year than they would have had you waited until you were sixty-six. (This example assumes you took payouts right upon turning sixty-two. If you take payments

Year of Birth*	Full Retirement Age	Age 62 Reduction Months	Total % Reduction
1937 or earlier	65	36	20.00
1938	65 and 2 months	38	20.83
1939	65 and 4 months	40	21.67
1940	65 and 6 months	42	22.50
1941	65 and 8 months	44	23.33
1942	65 and 10 months	46	24.17
1943–1954	66	48	25.00
1955	66 and 2 months	50	25.84
1956	66 and 4 months	52	26.66
1957	66 and 6 months	54	27.50
1958	66 and 8 months	56	28.33
1959	66 and 10 months	58	29.17
1960 and later	67	60	30.00

* Persons born on January 1 of any year should refer to the previous year.

early—starting at sixty-three, say, or sixty-four and a half—you'll still get reduced payments but at not so hefty a percentage; it's prorated, fairly scaled.)

In other words, the longer you live, the more you therefore penalize yourself by taking early payments.

If you're having a difficult time figuring out whether you should take the payments early, you can talk to a Social Security Administration representative who will answer more of your questions and help you think through the scenarios. The toll-free number is 1-800-772-1213, and as of this writing you can actually speak to a human being from seven A.M. to seven P.M. on business days.

FREQUENTLY ASKED QUESTIONS

Since this book hasn't yet contained any get-rich-quick formulas (c'mon, guys!), I now realize that I'll be working much longer than I'd originally thought. I have heard this can reduce my Social Security. . . .

If you wait to take Social Security at the normal appointed hour of your "full retirement age," as of the year 2000 going forward you get all your Social Security with no—we repeat, *no*—limit imposed due to any future earnings. Uncle Sam smiles and says, "Work." You want it in Monopoly terms? "Go directly to work, and *do* collect $200."

For those taking benefits before the age of sixty-five, there are special conditions, so consult the www.ssa.gov website or let your fingers do the walking.

My husband and I both worked. Do I get a better deal by taking my own entitlement or piggybacking on his?

Spouses who both qualify for Social Security each get paid a benefit. In the majority of cases, the husband has earned more than the wife, meaning the wife can choose whether to get paid the Social Security to which she's entitled or piggyback on her spouse's benefits. A spouse will always draw on his or her own work record first. Then any excess benefits from the partner will be paid by the partner's employer. This is done rather automatically, with the spouse in question getting upgraded to whichever is a better payout.

I was a stay-at-home parent who got divorced a few years ago. Do I qualify for any Social Security?

The magic number here is ten. If you were married for ten years or more, you'll get your ex-spouse's benefits. If not, not.

If you get remarried, you will typically sacrifice your entitlements to your former spouse's Social Security (though this is not the case if you remarry at age sixty or later—fifty, if disabled). We humbly suggest that love is a stronger force than eligibility requirements for your ex's Social Security, so get married! In fact, if this marriage fails, you can requalify for your first spouse's Social Security.

Everyone's situation is different, and we definitely won't cover every unique situation here. In addition to the phone number mentioned earlier (page 111), you can go into a local Social Security office and discuss your situation with a representative. The SSA website has a helpful locator to find your nearest office: http://www.ssa.gov/locator/. If you choose to go this route, get those papers in order: The Social Security site suggests you bring a picture ID, your and your former spouse's Social Security numbers, a marriage certificate, and a divorce decree.

We are a married couple. When one of us dies, does the other get the benefits?

If a widow or widower is at full retirement age (sixty-five to sixty-seven, depending) or older, she or he will get 100 percent of the deceased's Social Security. For those nearing retirement age (sixty to sixty-four), you'll get 70 to 95 percent of the benefits your spouse would have received. Regardless of your age, if you are a widow or widower with a child under sixteen, you'll get 75 percent of your spouse's Social Security. And finally, if there are no surviving parents, such benefits go directly through to children under the age of eighteen.

You may have your own benefits coming later, but if you begin getting your spouse's payments as a result of early death, you can take those in whatever form they presently exist and then supplant those in the future with your higher, better benefits.

If this topic is relevant to you, grab a copy of Publication No. 05-10084 (who numbers these things?) entitled "Social Security—Survivors Benefits."

Hey, I'd forgo all benefits from all I've ever paid in if I could opt out now!

We certainly feel this. So do many of our 2.2 million Motley
(continued)

Fool members, and so will increasing numbers of Americans going forward. It's inevitable: The younger you are, the stronger your feeling on the subject. Even many middle-aged people who've paid in for years and aren't far from a payout passionately wish they could opt out.

Why? It's not hard to figure. Americans are doing the math! They are coming to realize they will likely pay in more than they'll ever get back. Further, because of the increasing awareness and care being taken by many Americans to plan their own retirement (helped by the advent of tax-deferred IRA plans—particularly the Roth IRA—plus the spread of financial education, etc.), many feel greater degrees of financial independence largely by dint of their own hard work.

Were the desire to opt out a drumbeat, it would be getting a little bit louder and faster with each passing day. Optimists that we are, it's nevertheless hard for us to envision a resolution that will have every reader of this book walking away happy. Thus, it's better to focus on what will probably happen and allow each of us to connect the dots to see how it would affect us.

What changes to the system are likely, and by when?

The poet T. S. Eliot closed "East Coker," the second of his *Four Quartets,* with this oft-quoted line: "In my end is my beginning." That line was penned in 1940—the very year that Social Security began its first monthly payments to qualifying Americans. We're pretty sure Eliot didn't have FDR's newly born program in mind. But the parallel timing seems fairly labeled "poetic justice."

Why?

Because we believe that in time, Social Security should and must return to its original purpose: that of retirement insurance, not retirement benefits.

In 1940, 222,000 people received Social Security. Today, according to the sixty-fifth-anniversary Social Security pamphlet, 45 million people receive benefits. In fact, *one out of three is not even a retiree.* The pamphlet presents this as an achievement, which we consider ironic.

Earlier in this chapter, we were using quotation marks to point up that term "retirement benefits." That's because we think it's a euphemism that will fall apart. The original purpose of Social Security was as a safety net for a minority of elderly American retirees who would live past average life expectancy and need the money. It's only over time that Americans began to view it as a pension plan. But Social Security is not sustainable as a pension plan. That's why our prediction is that it will return in time to retirement *insurance.* So "retirement benefits" deserves quotation marks, since it seems to the common Fool an unstable euphemism.

At the time Social Security was first paid out, something on the order of forty workers were paying taxes to support each beneficiary. That number has declined today to about three workers paying taxes per retiree. With the "graying of America," this number is forecast to be two workers per retiree. Think about that: If we're to continue the system as is, and the average retiree is drawing down about $11,000 a year, half of that will be paid by American business (the corporate part of the equation) and the other half, coming to almost $3,000 each, will be transferred (paid) by the average worker. And that's Social Security taxes alone each year, to say nothing of income tax, property tax, capital-gains tax, etc.

So what happens? The ways out of this conundrum are few. As with the problems of Medicare and Medicaid covered in the last chapter, almost any solution must include either raising taxes or lowering benefits or both. Higher taxes to make more transfer payments are not the stuff of good economics, since the incentive to work and to produce are reduced at exactly the wrong time, i.e., when fewer people, in relative terms, are working. We believe the prospect of raising such taxes would severely hurt America. Whether higher Social Security taxes become politically acceptable is an interesting question, since a larger number of older voters could vote away more of the dollars of the outnumbered young. Yet we believe Americans are savvy to this and will not back politicians promoting the idea of raising Social Security taxes.

Which leaves reducing benefits.

Now, that isn't something many people would vote for in a vacuum, or on principle, is it? No one likes to see something that was promised taken away. Yet once you frame the discussion by asking, "How do we get out of this mess?" instead of "How much am I going to get?," you realize that this solution is the most feasible. Politicians trying to get elected won't want to take either of these stances (raise taxes versus lower benefits), but if the electorate forces them to come up with a solution, this path will be least resistance.

Think of it this way: The program was designed to pay out insurance to Americans living past the average life expectancy. Let's pretend for a second, with the poet, that truly its end were in its beginning:

For the year 2000, the National Center for Health Statistics quoted an average life expectancy at 76.9 years of age for all Americans at birth. (You may be interested to learn that in the year 2000, the average life expectancy for those who had made it to sixty-five was 17.9 more years, or about eighty-three.) So let's take that 76.9 figure, round it to 77, and to that *add the five years that were originally added to the late-1930s life expectancy.* We have reached a new trigger age at which you would begin receiving Social Security: eighty-two. You see, part of the problem is that after mandating payments at sixty-five, Congress hasn't seen fit to continually raise that age over the decades as it was rising in the real world. So a reformed Social Security, in adherence to the spirit of the original program, with comparable ranges set forth, would have Americans getting Social Security if and when they reach eighty-two years of age.

Will that happen? Could the government exhibit the equanimity necessary to make such a reform? We think not. There is virtually no likelihood that the retirement age necessary for payout will rise to eighty-two anytime soon. Further, while our age expectancy is up, and our general health along with it, we are not necessarily fitter to work today at seventy-seven than we were early last century. (Though it's not impossible, given our own family experience.)

However, no ifs, ands, or buts, we do believe the trend is clear: *The age should and will continue to go up,* probably more markedly than in the past, to fit better into today's world and today's life expectancy. The failing economics of Social Security will be a driving force leading to this solution.

Thus, much probability for higher retirement age.

Another way we'll probably be forced to reduce benefits is to move toward more need-based payouts. Like it or not, those of us who have been paying in to the system and don't truly need the money to retire or live on—many of whom do receive checks—will wind up getting less or even nothing from Social Security. In other words, Social Security will be returning more to insurance than pension. Part of what makes this tenable is that younger generations—over whom the sword of Damocles hangs, courtesy of previous administrations' economic decisions—are being told not to rely on Social Security. Theirs is the generation of ubiquitous tax-deferred plans like IRAs and 401(k)s.

Anyway, we think it highly likely that the percentage of the population qualifying for Social Security insurance must and will decline, with those who can most afford the sting getting stung.

Finally, expect these changes to occur incrementally. What this means for your retirement planning is that Social Security will continue in some form for the foreseeable future, shifting over time to the domain of those who really need it, something that looks much closer to the Medicaid crowd rather than middle-class America.

Which means in its end *is* its beginning.

Action Plan

■ Contact the Social Security Administration and get a copy of the document that details how much you can expect to receive from Social Security in your retirement.

■ Take a look at www.ssa.gov for any special situations. Were we to address every question or situation, you'd have in your hands a really, really boring book. Instead, read SSA's really, really boring—and yet incredibly comprehensive and very helpful—website. Examples of questions answered there are:

What are the disability requirements for an adult?
How long must you be married to collect benefits when a
    spouse dies?
Can a child born outside of marriage be entitled to benefits?
How do I contact the Railroad Retirement Board?
    (Supposing you'd want to!)

■ Yep, you name it. If you have a question, they have an answer. And if you're not Internet-inclined, most of the questions answered on the website are also available as documents you can request and read.

■ Do not count on Social Security as a retirement benefit that will last forever. More likely, it will return to being retirement insurance. Related to that: Do not predicate your retirement on retirement insurance. Take the other steps we provide in this book and improve your retirement income as best as you can, attempting to make any Social Security you do get just the cream, not the main course.

■ If you find yourself burning with a desire to learn even more about Social Security, get your hands on a copy of Lita Epstein's *The Complete Idiot's Guide to Social Security.*

■ Social Security is a hot topic on Capitol Hill. If you have any thoughts or concerns about it, share them with your representatives in Washington. You can do so very easily online, at www.congress.org.

Chapter Eleven

What to Do with Your Parents

Old age ain't no place for sissies.
—BETTE DAVIS

ONE OF THE tricks practiced by fate on the middle-aged is that the time when Junior has graduated from college can also be, to the surprise of many, the time when Dad falls and breaks his hip, and when you're confronted with the growing needs of your parents.

Most of us want the best for our parents, always. But it's often not so simple. They can come to need you more when you're beginning to enjoy a respite after raising your own children. That might seem like a raw deal, but stop and think about it, and you'll realize it's just the age-old contract we're born in to. Your parents cared for you and sacrificed for you when you were helpless (and later, helplessly adolescent). At the other end of your life, the time comes for you to do the same for them. The same will be done for you.

Consider this: It's not so unusual for people to spend more years caring for their parents than they did raising their children! (With technological progress come longer lifetimes—the Census Bureau expects there to be more than eight hundred thousand centenarians in 2050.)

Caring for aging parents can be very difficult. It may even feel like unrequited altruism until you pause and consider again: *Your children are watching.* Whether you like it or not (we hope you like it), they will one day model their own attention to you, their aging parent, based largely on the care and attention you bring to your parents.

Inspiration enough for this daunting chapter of our book and your life?

Great.

We've assembled tips, advice, and resources for you. Many of these relate to parents who need care now: good news for the weary. But even if your mater and pater are a decade or two away from such straits, it's still good to learn what to expect and how to be prepared.

GET ON THE SAME PAGE—EARLY

You should begin doing the first task early—ideally, while your parents are still thriving and active. If you put this off, you may end up with a parent suddenly incapable of telling you what you want or need to know.

Have some frank discussions.

Gather important information and learn their wishes—ideally, with your siblings present as well. Here's what you should tackle:

- ■ **Have your parents show you where they keep all their important documents.** Find out where their safe-deposit box is and the key. If they have a stash of expensive jewelry or gold coins, find out where it is. If they have a safe in the basement, ask how to open it. Have them list all their important accounts and account numbers. See if they'll tell you how much money they have invested here and there. One day you will need to know about every bank account, every brokerage account, every insurance policy, the mortgage or deed to any house, their wills and law firm that keeps the wills, burial arrangements and cemetery plots, etc. Don't let all this information stay only in one place, where a fire or other disaster might wipe it out. Keep a list of information in a safe backup place. If this sounds like a hassle, it is. But it will be much more of a hassle later if you don't prepare and attend to it now. If your parents are not cooperative, perhaps explain how this will make things easier on you later (emphasize *much later,* if that's helpful).

■ **Come to an understanding of their final wishes, such as funeral arrangements.** Jot down any preferences they have, perhaps regarding the kind of service they want, songs to be sung, the kind of casket, etc. Discuss whether they want to be organ donors and what their preferences are regarding life support if they end up in bad shape in a hospital. This is depressing stuff for anyone to think about, and it might make your parents even glummer. So you might make it more of a family affair by sharing your own wishes and preferences. This is sensible; terrible though it may be, you could conceivably die first, and your loved ones will want to know what *your* wishes were. Although the main purpose of this exercise is respect and the comfort that comes from being prepared rather than frantic, it's also likely that it will save some money as well. If you never discuss your father's funeral wishes with him, you might end up buying him a top-of-the-line casket, because anything less would seem disrespectful. But via a talk, your dad might explain that a simple inexpensive casket is fine by him. Maybe you'll learn that your mother would rather be cremated than buried. That can save money, too. When you're done with this discussion, do the Motley Fool thing and treat one another to ice-cream sundaes all 'round!

■ **Have them look into long-term care insurance if they haven't already done so.** We suggested this at the close of Chapter 9, but it's worth mentioning again that any middle-class American over the age of sixty-five who lacks long-term care insurance should be researching and looking to buy such a policy pronto. Increasing old age can make such insurance prohibitively expensive.

■ **Make sure your parents' various accounts are set up in a way best for all.** For example, if your mother isn't a *joint* owner of some financial accounts and then your dad dies, it may be a hassle for her to get access to the assets. If she's a joint owner, then ownership will automatically rest with her. See which beneficiaries have been listed for various accounts. On very old accounts, you might not have been listed, as you would have been too young. Update the beneficiaries to reflect your parents' current wishes.

■ **Discuss living arrangements.** At some point they probably won't be able to or won't want to live in their current home. What will they prefer then, and what can they or you afford? An apartment in an assisted-living facility? (As we mentioned earlier, tour a place or two, so you all have an idea of what they offer.) A smaller house near one of your siblings? Might they move in with you?

Don't expect to clear up every matter with your parents in one sitting. Some topics are kind of huge or complex or sad. Once you start the discussion, give your parents time to keep thinking about them, to possibly do some research of their own, to talk about these issues with their friends and perhaps see what their friends are planning on doing. If they're reluctant to give you all the details on their finances, perhaps they could still make up the lists but store them with a trusted friend or lawyer. Or maybe they could seal the information in an envelope they give you, with explicit directions to not open it until their death(s).

Perhaps this goes without saying, but while you're engaged in all these serious discussions, you might want to take some time to say how much you love one another. Why? Because these are the kinds of things that people often regret never saying to their loved ones. Here's some advice offered by Motley Fool member Claire on our discussion boards, to someone with an ailing father:

> Clear up any unfinished business with your dad, if he's still able to communicate with you . . . Any positive or loving message you want him to know. Don't rehash the negative, or bring up past issues—except to let him know that whatever it is, it is behind you—but say essentially that he shouldn't give any unhappy times between you another thought. More important, remind him of your love, your gratitude for having him to raise you, the good memories which you're going to treasure and pass on, and reassure him that he did a good job with you, and that you and yours are going to be just fine.

Also from that board, Motley Fool member Margaret listed some things her dad did and didn't do:

Potentially difficult things my dad took care of:

- Expressed very clearly to more than one person his feelings about various end-of-life interventions, extraordinary care, withdrawal of life support, etc.
- Told all of his children how much he loved them and how proud he was
- Made his peace with God and received the Anointing of the Sick (important to Catholics)
- Told me where he'd kept all his writings on the computer and encouraged me and my sibs to read them if we wanted

A few things I wish my parents had taken care of together before Dad died:

- Get all relevant papers in one place, including birth certificate, military discharge, Social Security, cemetery deed, will/living trust, etc.
- Decide on a burial location: Although my dad was terminally ill, apparently my mom didn't consider this until we were planning the wake and funeral
- Update the will to reflect current financial and family situation
- Get a handle on finances—how much money is in 401(k)/pension/IRA? How much life insurance? How much are property taxes and maintenance? What are tax implications? Etc.

GET EMPOWERED: LEGAL DOCS

Are you as tired of the word "empowerment" as we are? Forgive us, because in this case you *do* need to get empowered—literally. There are some *legal matters* your parents should take care of now. (And hey, if you're not already, you should get empowered, too, even if you're in your thirties.)

First off, your parents need to prepare a durable power of attorney document. A durable power of attorney designates someone (perhaps you, perhaps someone else) to attend to your parents' finances and make important decisions should they become incapacitated temporarily or permanently. Without this form in place, you might have to go through a lot of headaches, legal processes, and dollars, trying to get authorized to make decisions. Again, it's also smart for *you* to have such a power granted to someone should you become unable to do so—none of us knows when we might need that.

Next up, your parents (yet again, you, too) should have a health-care proxy (aka medical proxy) and living will (or advance directive) drawn up. These will specify who is to make important medical decisions and will record your parents' wishes in regard to life support, resuscitation, and so-called heroic measures undertaken at a hospital. Fail to have these documents in place, and you may end up in some agonizing situations.

Finally, make sure your parents have wills prepared and have done any necessary estate planning. If they dutifully drafted a will years ago, great. Find out where it's kept, perhaps with which lawyer. If it was drafted many years ago, it could probably stand to be updated.

Skip ahead to Chapter 14 right now if you'd like a more in-depth look at trusts and estates.

SOME OUNCES OF PREVENTION

To a degree, much of this aging stuff is out of your control. But you *can* do a few things to make your and your parents' lives easier.

First, go to the doctor! Regularly. This applies to both you and your parents. In your case, if you avoid it or put it off, you may end up with something serious that hampers your ability to care for your parents (and worse, that hampers your ability to live a full life!). If your parents avoid it or put it off, they may end up seriously (or terminally) ill much earlier than any of you expected. Caring for a dying eighty-nine-year-old parent isn't fun, but caring for a dying sixty-three-year-old parent is a lot sadder. If your parents are reluctant to go to the doctor, try offering to go with them. Perhaps make the appointment for them and take them.

Exercise. If your folks aren't already physically active, convince them that they need a *little* exercise in their lives. Studies have shown that the smallest amount of exercise you can imagine is better than nothing, and as little as a half hour of brisk walking every day or two can make a big difference in general overall health and diminishing your chances of contracting various diseases.

Next is a safety check. Remember how you baby-proofed your home, if you were ever blessed with little ones? Well, how about examining your parents' living quarters to see if any reasonable changes need to be made to enhance safety? You might, for example, attach a bar or handle to the wall next to the bathtub for them to hold on to, should they need to. Eager beavers could even scope out a store or two that sells products for the disabled. It might mortify your parents to think of such a thing, but as they get older, having something to grab on to here or there could come in handy and perhaps save them from a life-changing fall. (Remember, the bathroom is the most dangerous room in the house.) Preventive measures include affixing no-slip rubber strips to the bathtub or shower floor, removing any throw rugs that someone might slip on, lowering the temperature of the hot-water heater, making sure smoke detectors are in place and working, and looking for fire hazards throughout the house, such as overtaxed outlets or newspapers piled next to heaters. You might even look into taking a CPR course; it might come in handy.

And by the way, how is Mom's hearing? If it's been getting bad, have it checked. She might need a hearing aid to be able to hear the smoke alarm or doorbell. If she's having trouble with the telephone, get her one with adjustable volume. There are special telephones designed to help the hard of hearing.

Finally, ask if you can offer or arrange for any help for your parents. Your dad might take pride in still shoveling snow off the driveway, for example, but that's a common cause of heart attacks in older men. Help might come in the form of a shoveling service, a landscaping service, a handyman who's a phone call away, or perhaps a housecleaning service to tackle heavy work such as vacuuming or scrubbing floors. (There are services that will deliver meals to the elderly, for a fee or for free.) Simply locating a neighborhood teen who's interested in earning some money could be useful: He or she could change lightbulbs or mow the lawn. We're not suggesting you take away autonomy or vigorous activity from your parents' lives. We *are* suggesting that you and they think through how best their energies are spent, including avoiding common hazards for the elderly.

We've presented a rather thoroughgoing portrait of what you can do for your parents' health and safety. In the middle of living life ourselves, we know you have a life to live, too. Just do what you can manage. Any little step is a positive contribution.

LOOK FOR SIGNS, AND THEN TAKE ACTION

Sometimes the need to care for your parents hits you like a ton of bricks—such as if they suffer a heart attack or a stroke. Other times, though, the need for elder care can creep up on you. As your parents age, get in the habit of looking for signs. For example:

- Changes in your parents' appearance, demeanor, or personality. These could be signs of medical problems. (If your dad was always a snappy dresser and now he's neglecting to even brush his hair, something may be up.)
- Mail unattended to. Okay, Okay, we admit to ignoring *our* mail from time to time—three quarters of it is usually junk, after all! Nevertheless, if your parents' bills aren't getting paid, then utilities might get turned off, or worse, insurance policies canceled.
- Memory loss. We confess again that we already can't remember what we had for lunch yesterday. But if you find your parents consistently forgetting simple words, having trouble doing simple things they've done a million times, or losing track of the time, the day, or where they are, these can signal health problems and should be checked out by a doctor.
- Deteriorating driving skills. This point is critical, because it doesn't involve just the lives of your parents. It also can affect the lives of countless strangers who might be in danger if your parents are driving when they no longer should. So let Dad or Mom do the driving sometime, and if you feel convinced they shouldn't

be driving anymore, suggest or insist that they have their eyes and reflexes tested by a doctor. A poor performance may be all the ammo you need. If they refuse to give up driving when you insist they must, here's a hardball solution proposed by Jacqueline Marcell in her book, *Elder Rage, or Take My Father . . . Please!: How to Survive Caring for Aging Parents.* If the doctor thinks a parent should no longer drive, get a letter to that effect and send it to the DMV, asking them to take your parent's license away. Sneaky, yes? Have we done this for our parents? Fortunately, they haven't reached that age yet, and it will be our wish never to do anything like this. But if you determine that your parents' driving is becoming a matter of life or death for unwitting others, the end justifies the means. And the means may be somewhat less humiliating for your stubborn parent, since at least the decision would come from someone else, an impersonal government agency at that.

Need we point out that while you're keeping an eye on your mom and dad, you should most of all take the time to enjoy having them around, too? One day they won't be there anymore. Consider videotaping some talks with them about your family's history.

MONEY MATTERS

Your parents supported you financially for a long time. If they are not presently able to support themselves, you can help. For starters, know that as of 2003 you can give tax-free gifts to family members of up to $11,000 each. So if you and your spouse are helping support both your parents, *each* of you can give *each* of them up to $11,000 for a total of $44,000 per year (if you're lucky enough to afford to be so generous). That's not a deduction for you, but it *is* tax-free income for them.

If you're providing over 50 percent of your parents' support, and if you qualify by meeting certain other requirements, then you can claim your parents as dependents, which can be a financial benefit to you by providing a deduction on your tax return.

If you can set up a flexible spending account through your employer (covered in Chapter 9), you may be able to sock money into it to pay for expenses related to caring for your parents with pretax dollars. Track down someone in your human-resources office and ask about this.

If your parents don't like the idea of taking money from you, and they plan to leave you their home when they die, you might set up a reverse mortgage with them. Reverse mortgages, which provide payouts over time in exchange for eventual ownership of the house, are sold by various financial institutions and have various benefits and drawbacks. But you might set up a less formal one with your parents: You give them a set amount each month or year in exchange for the home upon their death. Win-win. (Well, except for the death part.)

HEALTH CARE

Chapter 9 already focused on this important topic for baby boomers; the same goes doubly for your parents.

What kind of health insurance do your parents have, and what is covered? Find out ahead of time what Medicaid will provide in the state where they live, and whether they'll qualify. In many cases, Medicaid kicks in only if a person has $3,000 or less in assets and his or her spouse has less than between $16,000 and $80,000 in assets and little to no income. Learn more about what your parents can and can't expect.

These kinds of issues and the planning they require are sometimes complex. This is a perfect time to consult a financial advisor (see Chapter 7), and if you've already found one you like, share the wealth! He or she can suggest asset- and estate-management techniques that should help your parents keep more of their money in the family and spend less of it unnecessarily.

Remember again to consider Medigap insurance, the private insurance you buy to fill in the holes between what Medicare covers and what you can afford. Medigap comes in many flavors; your friendly local insurance agent will probably be more than happy to help you find the most lickable.

Here are some typical health-care costs that face many aging parents, from *Ernst & Young's Financial Planning for Women:*

- Nursing home: $36,000–$72,000 per year
- Continuing care retirement community: $2,000 per month (after initial fee)
- Assisted living: $1,000–$2,000 per month
- Adult day care: $40–$70 per day
- Registered nurse: $30–$50 per hour
- Home care worker: $10–$14 per hour

And now for some scary statistics:

- At sixty-five the average person's chances of being admitted to a nursing home at some point in the future are more than four in ten. (Source: Long Term Care Campaign)
- One person in three who turned sixty-five in 1990 will stay a year in a nursing home. One person in ten will stay five years or more. (Source: National Association of Insurance Commissioners)
- In 1994, 7.3 million Americans needed long-term care services at an average cost of nearly $43,800 per year. By 2000 this number rose to 9 million Americans at nearly $55,750 per year, and due to inflation, by 2060 it will skyrocket to 24 million Americans paying over $250,000 per year to receive long-term care. (Source: Long Term Care Insurance National Advisory Council)
- In line with numbers quoted earlier, recent studies report that out of every five people age sixty-five and over, two will enter a nursing home and stay an average of 2.5 years. (Source: *Life Insurance Selling,* December 1995)
- Within a year after admission as private-pay residents, 90 percent of nursing-home residents are impoverished. (Source: *How to Protect Your Life Savings,* by Harley Gordon et al., 1995)

Please note: There's still a good chance your parents may never need any long-term care services. But odds are, one of them will. With proper planning and foresight, you can prepare yourself and your parents financially for such possible needs.

In the meantime, consider this advice from Arleen, a member of our Fool Community online:

> At my aunt's funeral, my cousin said she'd one day told her, "Well, you're not dead yet, so let's spend whatever time we have left doing whatever you're able. We'll go through old photos, reminisce about times we've had, watch favorite movies together—whatever you feel up to." And they did. This was by far the best advice I could have ever been given, because it's shown me how to talk to anyone who's terminally ill. They're not dead yet. Treat them like they're still alive!

GET HELP—YOU'LL NEED IT

Don't take everything on your shoulders. For starters, enlist the help and cooperation of family if you can; perhaps a cousin or sibling can take over a few days a week or month. If your parents don't live near you, in addition to calling them regularly, you might find a neighbor who will agree to look in on them, be your eyes and ears to the extent necessary. We can't emphasize this enough: Involve other family members.

If caring for your parent(s) becomes a major burden, consider joining or forming a support group to help you deal with the stress and frustrations. Too many people think they're alone in a situation when someone down the street might be going through the same experiences. (Heck, there are support groups for aging parents themselves!) There are more than 20 million Americans caring for aging parents, and that number is growing. For support and advice online, drop by our "Baby Boomers" discussion board at Fool.com (http://boards.fool.com/messages.asp?bid=112954).

If you lack family, another helper comes in the form of your local social services department. For example, you may be able to arrange for your mom to be driven to doctor's appointments or have meals delivered to her.

Again, consider consulting a financial advisor to plan how you'll deal with current and future needs of your parents.

DON'T FORGET DIGNITY

Perhaps the least desirable situation has you caring for parents who have become as helpless as children. If so, don't let yourself fall into the habit of treating them like children. In fact, no matter how with(out) it your parents are, try to always be calm and patient. Getting old is no picnic for them, either. Losing one's independence can be extremely difficult. Respect them and their wishes as much as possible. Involve them as much as you can in discussions and plans related to their care. Remain their loving son or daughter, and don't let yourself become patronizing.

FOR FURTHER THINKING

*Comedian Ben Stein on what he learned from
his father, Herb Stein:*

Tom: Your father, Herb Stein, went to Williams at the age of fifteen, as we understand it.
Stein: Yes. He was the same age roughly that my son is in eighth grade.
Tom: (*Laughter.*) Okay. Your father went on to become a professionally accomplished economist serving as the chairman of the Council of Economic Advisers. What was the primary lesson your dad taught you about money?
Stein: Well, that money is a scarce good. That money is not to be treated lightly. I still spend a lot of it frivolously, but I also save a lot. My father taught me a great lesson. He said he had learned it from Bernard Baruch, and it is that in any situation, in any economic climate, there is no substitute for working and saving. I am so blessed that he taught me to save. I live in a world of incredible uncertainty. I don't know when my show is going to be canceled. I don't know when people aren't going to want me to give speeches.

DON'T GET OVERWHELMED

Finally, for those self-sacrificers among us, or for any who find themselves mired in an endless routine of caring for aging parents, *do take time off for yourself.* You can't be an effective and dutiful son or daughter if you don't take breaks to recharge your own batteries. Plus, you don't want to neglect the others in your life who want your company and attention, like your family, your friends, your dog. Take care of yourself so you can take care of others.

And do occasionally remind yourself how lucky you are, when you think about it, to have one or both parents live so long. Some final thoughts for you from Fool Community member Gayle:

> My parents died when I was twenty and twenty-one. My grandmother, however, lived to ninety-four, and I took care of her, although she was in assisted living. These are not financial suggestions, they are quality-of-life ideas.
>
> I made sure to take her out shopping (and that nearly drove me over the edge and ruined my back from lifting her wheelchair into the trunk), and I held a number of small dinner parties for her with six or eight of her friends at my house and just acted as maid and let her be the hostess. The southern-belle hostess in her emerged with gusto each time we did this.
>
> I also held birthday parties for her and invited all her friends. Even went so far as to have a Kermit the Frog come to the party and serenade her with songs "he" had made up with tidbits of information I provided about her. She *loved it!* Why an eighty-nine-year-old woman loved Kermit, I'll never know, but she did and turned positively coquettish. Maybe it was the margaritas I smuggled into her room and served her and the guests.
>
> Additionally, I made Christmas cookies and caramel corn and pralines and put them on small plastic or straw plates and wrapped them with red cellophane. Took a couple of dozen of those to her the first or second week in December every year so that she had something to give anyone who dropped in or gave her a gift.
>
> That's about it. Regarding parents, I'd say that as hard as it may be to make the sacrifices of time, energy, and finances, people should be thankful their parents are still around to collect the divi-

dends of all the love and caring they deposited when their children were growing up. I'd trade with those folks in a second. My parents have been dead thirty and almost thirty-one years, and I miss them every day.

Action Plan

Here's a short list to help get you thinking through—and enacting—good care for aging parents:

■ Talk! Talk with your parents, with your siblings, and with any friends who are grappling with these issues. Consult a financial advisor. Have your parents talk to their advisors and friends, so that they're part of the process and not treated as children. Discuss their preferences and wishes regarding how they want to live as they become less able to care for themselves. Discuss end-of-life issues. Discuss financial arrangements and insurance coverage. Don't put off these talks until it's too late.

■ Learn as much as you can so that you're comfortable with how you'll process what life deals you and your parents. Learn about services available to them now and later, such as Medicare.

■ Take advantage of the many resources listed below. Some can help you plan now, and others may be of use as your parents age and you begin to make various arrangements.

Resources

How to Care for Aging Parents, by Virginia Morris
Taking Care of Aging Family Members: A Practical Guide, by Wendy Lustbader and Nancy R. Hooyman
The Complete Eldercare Planner: Where to Start, Which Questions to Ask, and How to Find Help, by Joyce Loverde
Children of Aging Parents: 800-227-7294
www.aahsa.org: The American Association of Homes and Services for the Aging (202-783-2242)
www.alfa.org: Assisted Living Federation of America (703-691-8100)
www.aoa.dhhs.gov: The government's Administration on Aging,

with information about opportunities and services available to enrich the lives of older persons and support their independence.

www.elderweb.com: Thousands of reviewed links to long-term care information, a searchable database of organizations, and an expanding library of articles and reports, news, and events. Learn more about hospitals, health care providers, laws and regulations, and many other issues related to the aging.

www.maxiaids.com: Products for independent living

www.medicare.gov: Get info from the horse's mouth, or call 1-800-633-4227

www.pueblo.gsa.gov: The Federal Citizen Information Center— free pamphlets from the government on scores of topics of interest to consumers (1-888-8-PUEBLO)

www.retirement-living.com: An online version of a free publication, with info on nursing homes, continuing-care communities, independent living, home health care, and adult day care centers.

www.seniorsites.com: "The most comprehensive Web source of nonprofit housing and services for seniors."

Yahoo!'s directory of resources for seniors: http://dir.yahoo.com/ Society_and_Culture/Cultures_and_Groups/Seniors/

Chapter Twelve

Paying for Your Kids and College

In the past the intrinsic pleasures of parenthood for most American families were increased by the extrinsic economic return that children brought. Today, parents have children despite their economic cost. This is a major, indeed a revolutionary, change.

—KENNETH KENISTON

DR. KENISTON, THIS must have something to do with love, and our compulsion to ape immortality, and our genes' overweening insistence on making guest appearances right down through the generations. Still, there's no way around it: Raising and educating children are an expensive proposition. Yet most parents seem to think that the benefits outweigh the (considerable) costs.

Financial planning for children doesn't have to freak you out. It's not impossible, and you *can* afford to send your children to college. So relax and let us give you a solid introduction to this topic, setting the stage for any further research you might want to do. Even if your children are already past college and into their adult lives, you may learn some useful things about how to save for your grandchildren's education (even if they're not yet born). Yes, we'll include a few tips at the end for those who find they're playing catch-up.

BAD NEWS FIRST: THE COSTS

Sorry to fling bad news toward you at what seems like regular intervals in this book. But at least we generally put the bad news up front.

Much of this chapter will revolve around college expenses, but let's make the obvious point that children can be costly, even setting aside higher-education bills. To prove it, consider Betsy Howie's book, *Callie's Tally: An Accounting of Baby's First Year (Or, What My Daughter Owes Me)*. Call it thorough or call it obsessive; we'll just call it revealing. Howie recorded the cost of every expense related to Callie, her newborn. Yup, every bottle, iron tablet, Pamper, and Peppermint Patty (for postpartum blues) is meticulously documented and categorized (e.g., breast-feeding expenses are filed under "groceries"). At the end of year one, Howie presents Callie with the grand total: $26,099.59 for all billed and nonbilled expenses (child care not included, thanks to Howie's on-call mom).

Callie does get a few freebies along the way. For example, in celebrating her first fiscal quarter, Mom throws a party at which her daughter is not billed for even one plastic fork. Callie collects credits as well, such as the "internment rebate"—a bonus for keeping Mom at home and out of the checkout lines.

Need we detail costs of children between crib and dorm room? Add up all the saxophone lessons and soccer balls and snow cones and summer camps? Nah . . . it's more important to focus on *how* you'll cover these bills. The answer lies in planning, saving, and investing.

(What, you thought there was another answer?)

THE GOOD NEWS: FINANCIAL SOLUTIONS

The good news is that you can handle the expenses of children, especially with financial discipline. Ideally, you'll start budgeting, saving, and investing as early as possible. The more time your money has to grow, the more it will grow, socked into a long-term growing vehicle such as the stock market. Consider these scenarios:

- Invest $2,000 per year beginning when your child is eight, and if you earn 8 percent annually, you'll end up with $29,000 by the time he's eighteen.
- Invest $5,000 per year beginning when your child is ten (earning 8 percent annually), and you'll have more than $53,000 by the time she's eighteen.
- Invest $3,000 per year at the same rate from the time of your child's birth, and by the time he's ready for college, you'll have a little more than $112,000.

These are just rough guidelines. If, during the years that you're investing, you earn the market's historical average return (around 10 percent), you'll have even more money. (Though over any relatively short period, such as five years, the market might slump.) Still, the rate of return on your money probably won't have as much impact as how much you save, how soon you start, and how many years your money is left to grow. So if you're not a Rockefeller (or a Winfrey or a Gates), you're not doomed. You just need to start as soon as possible. (If you are a grandparent, consider helping your kids by tossing a few coins into the college fund for their little fellers.) Start now!

KINDS OF INVESTMENTS

One question many people have is *where* to invest money for their children. The answer to that question is simple! It depends. Oh, you wanted more? Okay, it depends primarily on how old your children are and when you expect to spend the money. The longer the time period until you'll need the money, the more risk you can take. Here's a typical set of guidelines, based on the age of your children:

- Birth to school age: 100 percent growth stocks. You have more time, you can take more risk.

- Ages six to thirteen: 70 percent stocks, 30 percent bonds. You might want to think about making a few "safer" selections. Bonds are typically less volatile than stocks.
- Ages fourteen to eighteen: 30 percent bonds, 20 percent stocks, and 50 percent money-market funds. You want your money to grow, but you also want to protect yourself from market volatility.
- College age: 100 percent money-market funds. You need to be able to access the money easily and not have it drop in value. For funds earmarked to be spent a year or two down the road, certificates of deposit are a good idea.

This guide is just a rough one. You might want to take on more or less risk due to your circumstances or temperament. Also important are the vehicles through which you invest, such as brokerage accounts, tax-deferred accounts, etc. We'll put those in a headlock soon enough. But first, let's take a closer look at how you can make ends meet, then accumulate cash to invest.

IT'S ALL ABOUT SAVING

Saving may sound like a painful thing to do, but there are so many different ways to do it that surely some of them won't be too onerous. We've already given you eight games to play to reduce expenses and increase your savings. Not satisfied? Here are a bunch more ideas.

Consider quitting smoking, expensive coffee, or both. Cutting out one $7.75 pack of Lucky Strikes a day can net you tens of thousands of dollars down the road if those savings are invested. The same goes for the $3 coffee you might buy every morning. Just make coffee at home, and you'll save a bundle. Brown-bag your lunch a few times a week, and you can save $15 per week, or over $700 per year.

Consider public schooling. Precollege schooling is a big issue for many parents. Do you send your kids to a private elementary or high school in the hope of giving them the best education possible? Well, that's a fine thought, and we both went to great private schools (here's a shout-out to St. Alban's in Washington, D.C., and Groton and St. Mark's in Massachusetts). We greatly appreciate private education and are major proponents of it. But even we have to agree that you shouldn't overspend on elementary or high school if you won't have anything left over for college. At least consider sending Brittany and Taylor to public school, then enhancing that education in other ways, inexpensively. For instance, take them to the library, read to them, let them see you reading. Take them to museums, to other states and countries. Introduce them to strategy board games, opera, and volunteering. Think creatively, act purposefully, and you'll raise curious, well-rounded children, whatever the heck high school they went to.

Open your eyes to less expensive alternatives. Baby food, for example? Pretty pricey! But with a little effort (and a food processor), you can make your own. Grow some of your own vegetables and you'll save even more money. Instead of buying lots of new books for your tots, find them at garage sales, at www.half.com, or at your local library. Instead of hiring an expensive clown for a birthday party, or renting out some children's venue, have a good old-fashioned party at home, where you're the emcee running lots of games, such as pin-the-tail-on-the-donkey or guess-how-many-beans-are-in-this-jar. You might be surprised at how well it goes over.

Buy in bulk whenever it makes sense and costs less. This means shopping at discount warehouses. But the concept applies elsewhere, too. If you go to the zoo a few times a year, it might be cost-effective to buy an annual membership that will permit you to enjoy lions and tigers and bears more often.

Take advantage of free money. Yes, free money! You may find some at the office, if your employer is generous enough to match your contributions to a 401(k). (This will help your retirement more than it will pay for baby formula, but it's still free money.) Another option is to look for deals whenever you set out to buy something. At the supermarket, try to buy what you need when it's on sale, perhaps with coupons. If you're buying something online, first consult sites like www.dealcatcher.com, which tell you if, for example, Amazon.com is offering a special discount or free shipping.

Finally, the best advice on managing money that we can offer to those with children is: Get your children involved. Set up a family budget together, and let your kids know how much electricity and water cost, not to mention car payments. Teach them about investing, and buy them a few shares of stock when they're young. Teach them with their allowance or money they earn to save a portion for major expenses, to invest a portion, and to give away a portion to charity. If you are effectively doing this, guess what? As your kids get older, you can expect them to save for college along with you. If children appreciate the value of money and understand how it comes and goes, they'll squander less of it, and you'll have a lean, mean family machine.

A COLLEGE EDUCATION IS (SURPRISE, SURPRISE) VERY EXPENSIVE!

Are you ready to be hit in the face with a bucketful of cold water? According to the College Board, the average tuition cost for the 2002–2003 school year was $4,081 for a public four-year college and $18,273 for a private four-year college. Those price tags are up 9.6 percent and 5.8 percent, respectively, from the previous year, which demonstrates an enduring and frustrating aspect of college costs: Similar to medical costs, they have risen at a rate that has far outpaced inflation. It's getting to the point where if our food costs were rising with our college costs, by 2050 even a box of Cap'n Crunch would be too expensive for the several adults who (like one of your coauthors) still eat the cereal well past the time they were supposed to outgrow it. (David asserts that you can't prove he does this.)

Don't forget to factor in the cost of room and board and other expenses, typically around $8,000 per year. Your total tab will likely be between $12,000 and $27,000—*per year!* Multiply that by four, and you have a rough idea of what it would cost to give one cherub a college education today. (Keep in mind that some schools will cost a bit less and some a bit more.)

At this point, you might be looking for an oven to stick your head into. Don't! This cloud has several silver linings. Again from our friends at the College Board:

- 38 percent of students attending four-year schools pay under $4,000 for tuition and fees.
- Almost 70 percent of students attending four-year schools pay under $8,000 for tuition.
- A record $90 billion in financial aid is available to students and their families, an increase of over 11.5 percent from last year.
- At four-year *private* colleges and universities, over 75 percent of students receive some type of financial aid.
- At four-year *public* colleges and universities, over 60 percent of students receive some type of financial aid.

Feel better? We thought you would.

Your young 'uns don't necessarily have to be geniuses to earn scholarship money. At the end of this section, we'll provide some resources to help you zero in on dollars that might be sitting on a (non-craps) table near you. Too many people leave too much money on the table; don't be one of them. Here's a green-thumb preview: If little Susie loves to garden and participates in your local state garden club, she should apply for one of the scholarships handed out by the National Council of State Garden Clubs. They average $3,500! If she's a solo gardener, look into getting her more involved with local gardening organizations. Check to see if your or your spouse's employer offers any scholarships. You may be surprised. The McDonnell Douglas Scholarship Foundation, for example, gives up to $4,000 per year to selected children of its employees.

PUBLIC VERSUS PRIVATE

Armed with the information we've just given you, you may be warming up to the idea of sending young Hortense to State U. instead of Ivy College. That's not a bad idea. The debate over whether an education at an elite school translates into higher lifetime earnings rages on. Some studies have claimed that the cost of a highly selective and challenging school is justified by higher earnings. Others have found flaws in those studies' methodology. (Academics debating academics about academics—don't you love it?)

One study conducted by the National Bureau of Economic Research looked at students who were *accepted* at prestigious schools but chose to go somewhere else (so the study was looking at students with the same qualifications—in other words, bright and accomplished kids). The choice of school didn't affect earnings at all, except for those at the low end of the income scale. Students from lower-income families saw a small increase in lifetime earnings if they attended the more prestigious school, presumably because of better social networking opportunities. For most students, however, there was no meaningful difference.

An interesting exercise is to have your child interview five to ten adults whom he or she admires, asking where they went to college and how they think their choice made a difference in their career.

Your child might also look over the following lists of people and the schools they attended. Successful people have gone to all kinds of schools.

Public Schools

Warren Buffett	University of Nebraska
Katie Couric	University of Virginia
Stephen King	University of Maine
David Letterman	Ball State University
Colin Powell	City College of New York
Steven Spielberg	California State College
Oprah Winfrey	Tennessee State University

Private Schools

Carly Fiorina	Stanford University
Ruth Bader Ginsberg	Cornell University
Steve Jobs	Reed College
Condoleezza Rice	University of Denver
Tiger Woods	Stanford University

Either option could work out great. In fact, our own brotherly background backs this up: David went to a public school (the University of North Carolina—go Tar Heels!) while Tom went to a private school (Brown University—go Bears!). (D.G. note: Tom,

"Go Brown Bears"? That just doesn't have much of a ring to it. T.G. note: Well, that's because we're focused on *education* at Brown. D.G. note: So were we—and we couldn't take all our courses pass/fail! T.G. note: Really? I thought the only passes at North Carolina were on the hoops court. Etc.)

If your child already has a career in mind, then perhaps he or she should consider the top schools in that field. In many cases, the best schools are public. If you can get the best training for a public-college price, whadda bahggin.

FOR FURTHER THINKING

Loretta Lynn on what she wished she'd known when she first started:

David: What is the one thing you wish you knew about business back when you started this journey in 1960?

Loretta Lynn: That I would be away from my family so much. That is the one thing, if I had my life to do over, and I knew what I know now. But there is no way. You can't look back and say, "I wished I hadn't've done that." Because life goes on, and you are going to have to live it. But I would love to be with my little twins. They are on the road with me now.

SELLING COLLEGE TO YOUR KIDS

One issue that some parents of near-college-age children have to deal with is ambivalence about attending. Permit us to arm you with some statistics to use in getting your children to want to go to college.

The main reason is further education, of course. Whereas high school typically focuses on topics like social studies and language arts, in college your child can zero in on topics of real interest and can discover some new loves: astronomy, sociology, folklore, physics, economics, engineering, even ethnomusicology. College is also a great place to make a bunch of lifelong friends.

What might speak most to some teenagers is simply money. According to the U.S. Census Bureau, people who have earned a bachelor's degree earn over 80 percent more on average than those with only a high school diploma. The College Board notes, "Over a lifetime, the gap in earning potential between a high school diploma and a B.A. (or higher) is more than $1,000,000," adding, "What this boils down to is that whatever sacrifices you make for college in the short term are more than repaid in the long term."

Here's a chart to flash at your kids.

THE EARNING POWER OF EDUCATION		
EDUCATION LEVEL ACHIEVED	YEARLY SALARY	WEEKLY SALARY
Not a high school graduate	$22,074	$425
High school graduate only	$27,975	$538
Some college but no degree	$33,948	$653
Bachelor's degree	$51,644	$993
Master's degree	$61,296	$1,179
Ph.D.	$80,225	$1,543
Professional degree*	$95,175	$1,830

* Medical doctor, lawyer, etc.
(Median earnings, source: U.S. Census Bureau, 2000)

And finally, a warning. BEWARE ALL YE WHO TRAVEL HERE: Sharing with your young ones the eye-opening table above too repeatedly, or over too prolonged a period, may get them suddenly talking law school.

PLANNING AND SAVING FOR COLLEGE

And now we come to the main course.

With proper planning and disciplined investing, amazing things are possible as you save for college. For example: If, as soon as your child is born, you invest $100 a month and earn 8 percent per year, you'll have almost $50,000 in eighteen years (assuming you utilize a tax-friendly savings vehicle, which we'll discuss soon). That's $50,000 less that you or your child might have to borrow.

Let's jump into a discussion of the various tax-advantaged investment options. (Some of these apply to a wide range of educational costs—not just college.)

First up, the Coverdell ESA.

THE COVERDELL ESA

If you think you've never heard of the Coverdell ESA, you may be mistaken. It used to be called the Education IRA, though it was never an IRA in the familiar—retirement—sense of the term. In memory of the late senator Paul Coverdell (R-Ga.), it has a new moniker: the Coverdell Education Savings Account (ESA).

The Coverdell ESA allows for a maximum annual contribution of $2,000 per student. Just open an account with a bank, brokerage, or mutual-fund company, send in the contribution, and choose your investments. The earnings in the account grow tax-free as long as distributions are used for eligible expenses, which are not limited to college costs. The funds in a Coverdell can also be used to cover costs associated with attending elementary or secondary school, be it public, private, or religious. These costs include uniforms, computers, and transportation. (Sorry, Happy Meals and tuba camp are not yet eligible.)

A responsible person controls the account until the beneficiary reaches the age of majority (age eighteen in most states, even if your daughter is still prohibited from dating). The person in control of the account chooses the investments, which can be stocks, bonds, mutual funds, or cash equivalents.

Any individual may contribute a maximum of $2,000 a year to a

Coverdell ESA for the benefit of any person under age eighteen. But the contribution limit is phased out for contributors with a modified adjusted gross income between $95,000 and $110,000, for single persons, and between $190,000 and $220,000 for joint filers. (The phase-out is ratable; i.e., if you're single and your income is halfway between $95,000 and $110,000, then you can contribute $1,000—half of the maximum.)

If you exceed those income limits, don't worry. Just give the money to the child and let him open the Coverdell ESA himself.

For example, let's say Jocelyn, a single person, wants to establish a Coverdell ESA for her favorite little guy, Spanky. Problem (in this context, anyway): Jocelyn's adjusted gross income is $130,000. If you've been following along at home carefully, you know that her maximum contribution to little Spanky's Coverdell ESA will be zippo zero zilch, because of the income-limitation rules. But there is no reason that Jocelyn can't make a $2,000 gift to Spanky, who can then open his own Coverdell ESA, since he's well under the income limitations (assuming his lemonade stand doesn't rake in over $95,000 a year).

You have until the due date of your tax return (not including extensions) to make a contribution and still have it apply to the previous year.

Funds must be used by the time the beneficiary turns thirty. However, the account can be transferred to a relative (including cousins, step-relatives, and in-laws). If funds are used for an unqualified expense, earnings will be assessed a 10 percent penalty, and they'll count as ordinary income to the beneficiary.

Like any other investment account, Coverdell ESAs are offered by brokerage firms, mutual funds, and banks. Keep fees, commissions, choices of investment, and other features (phone trades, research products, local offices, etc.) in mind as you choose where to set up a Coverdell ESA.

Next up for your consideration are "529 plans." There are two types of these beasts: prepaid tuition plans and college savings plans. We'll tackle each separately.

529 PREPAID TUITION PLANS

Prepaid tuition plans became part of Section 529 of the Internal Revenue Code in 1996. (Are there sweeter words than "prepaid tuition"?) Through them, you buy a given number of tuition credits in a public college or university at today's prices. Regardless of tuition increases, the number of quarters/semesters/years purchased today is guaranteed for the future. The state agrees to pay those costs later, at whatever price that might be, but only if the student attends an in-state school.

Prepaid tuition plans should appeal to conservative investors, since they offer guaranteed tuition payments. The plans might also be a wise choice for students three to seven years away from college, because they should be playing it safe with such a short investment time horizon. However, since the risk of covering the rising costs of tuition is assumed by the plan, you'll pay a premium—you can't expect someone to take on a financial risk for nothing, can you? (Also, most prepaid tuition plans cannot be set up for the benefit of students who are beyond the ninth or tenth grade.)

Since it's hard to anticipate where a student will go to college, most states have provisions for using the savings to pay for tuition at a private or out-of-state school. However, states will not guarantee that the credits in your account will cover tuition at another school. Your contract will be valued based on the state's tuition rates, or you'll get back your contributions, with modest interest.

Some prepaid plans cover just tuition and fees; other plans will also pay for room and board. If you participate in a plan that does not cover room and board, you'll have to save separately for those expenses. As with the other college savings options, a prepaid tuition plan can be transferred to another family member.

Choosing a prepaid tuition plan can be simple: Does your state offer one? (Fewer than half do, as of this writing.) If it does, that may be your single option. Most programs are open only to contributors or future students who are residents.

529 COLLEGE SAVINGS PLANS

A 529 college savings plan is basically an investment account designed to help you save for college expenses. Unlike a 529 prepaid tuition plan, a 529 college savings plan does not lock in future tuition costs at today's prices. It affords an opportunity for investments to grow over the years at rates that equal—or, better yet, exceed—increases in costs.

Investments in a 529 savings plan grow tax-free as long as the money is used to pay for qualified higher-education expenses (tuition, fees, books, supplies, and room and board). While contributions to the 529 are not federally tax-deductible, some states permit a partial or complete state tax deduction to residents.

Anyone may contribute to a 529 plan. You don't even necessarily have to live in the state of the plan you choose. Let's make this plain: You could live in New Mexico and contribute to a plan based in Maine for your grandchild who lives in Oregon and ends up going to college in Michigan.

Got that?

By the way, if you're thinking of going back to school yourself, most plans will even allow you to set up your own 529 savings account.

The contribution limits to 529 plans are very high, over $200,000 in most cases. Most of the plans have no age or income limitations, so higher-bracket taxpayers can participate unfettered. Unlike a custodial account (e.g., Coverdell, Uniform Gift to Minors Act [UGMA], Uniform Transfer to Minors Act [UTMA], the assets in a 529 college savings plan remain in your control. With a few exceptions, your kids can't grab the money and run off to Europe when they reach the age of majority. You decide when distributions are made and what the funds will be used for. (At last, something you can lord over the kids after they turn eighteen!)

If you remove the earnings from a 529 plan and decide not to use them for higher-education expenses, you'll not only pay taxes on those earnings, you'll also get zapped with a 10 percent penalty. However, most 529 plans will allow you to change beneficiaries. So, if your child decides not to attend college, you can transfer the account to a new beneficiary who is directly related (siblings, cousins, step-relatives, and in-laws).

If these 529 plans are sounding practically perfect, they are. Practically, that is. A main drawback is their inflexibility. You can't directly manage the funds yourself; you must choose a money manager (think "mutual fund"). The number of investment options varies from plan to plan, ranging from a few funds to almost thirty. Once you've chosen your asset allocation, you can't change the mix for twelve months. If you're not happy with the 529 plan, you can transfer to another plan, but no more than once every twelve months.

Just about every state offers a 529 college savings plan. The quality of the plans and their rules and regulations vary dramatically. We can't emphasize how much these plans differ. For example, most plans allow the account owner to change beneficiaries, but some don't. Spend time getting to know what's out there. Unfortunately, since most of the plans are a few years old, they don't have an extensive history to evaluate. Also, since the 529 market is rapidly growing, expect significant changes in the coming years.

The best place to compare 529 plans is at www.savingforcollege.com, which offers a 529 plan evaluator and a rating for each plan. If you want a snapshot of all the plans, check out *Business Week*'s "Guide to College-Savings Plans" (to access it electronically, you'll have to take a deep breath and type the following address into your browser: www.businessweek.com/magazine/content/02_10/b3773602.htm).

Here are some things to look for when seeking the best plan:

■ Rules and restrictions you can live with: If you want to be able change beneficiaries, for example, make sure a given plan permits that.

■ Low expenses: Watch for enrollment fees, transfer fees, annual fees, and the annual expenses on the investments. Generally, we recommend that you don't consider plans with investments that charge over 1.5 percent a year, and you can find investments that charge much less. Also, depending on the plan, you may have to pay an up-front commission.

■ A variety of good investments: Some plans offer just a couple of ho-hum choices, whereas others offer a menu of more than twenty mutual funds. You want flexibility and respectable performance.

- Perks for residents: Since some states offer incentives for residents to choose their plan, like L. Frank Baum's Dorothy, you may not need to look any farther than your own backyard. Such incentives include state tax deductions, scholarships, and matching contributions. And your little dog, too!

"OKAY, FOOLS, SO WHAT'S BEST FOR ME?"

As you deliberate over these options, here are some pros and cons for each, prepared by crackerjack Fool staffer Robert Brokamp.

Why a prepaid tuition plan is right for you:

- You're risk-averse.
- You like knowing your tuition will be covered.
- You don't think you'll be eligible for financial aid. Unlike the other options, assets in a prepaid tuition plan reduce financial-aid eligibility dollar for dollar.

Why a prepaid tuition plan is wrong for you:

- It isn't offered by your state or by the school your child wants to attend.
- You prefer to choose your own investments.
- Your children are young, so the longer time horizon will allow you to be more aggressive with your investments, potentially resulting in more money.

If you'd rather use an investment account to fund your or your progeny's college education, then you have another choice to make: a Coverdell ESA or a 529 savings plan? Here are the most important considerations.

Why a Coverdell ESA is preferable:

- Distributions are tax-free. So are distributions from a 529 plan—until 2011. It's likely that Congress will extend the tax-free treatment of distributions, but it's not a sure thing.

- You choose the investments. You can invest in stocks, bonds, mutual funds, or plain old cash. With a 529 plan, you must choose a money manager. On top of that, since most 529 plans are relatively new, the accounts have short histories, making it difficult to evaluate their quality.

- Funds in a Coverdell ESA can also be used for eligible primary- and secondary-education expenses.

Why a 529 savings plan is preferable:

- The contribution limits on 529 plans are significantly higher.
- Your state may offer a tax deduction for contributions to the local 529 plan. Some states also offer other perks, such as scholarships and matching contributions.
- You might want to use the funds for educational purposes after the student turns thirty—the time by which funds in a Coverdell ESA must be used or transferred to a younger relative.
- A friend or relative wants to give a large amount to the student, perhaps as an estate-planning strategy. Furthermore, this magnanimous person can give more than the $11,000 annual limit on tax-free gifts—five times as much, in fact. Estate planning and gifting are complicated topics, so do some research before transferring such large amounts of money.

Fortunately, you can simultaneously contribute to a Coverdell ESA and both types of 529s. Why would you do this? Here are a few scenarios:

- You'd like to diversify. You want some of your money to lock in a portion of future tuition costs through a prepaid plan, but you also want to see if your investing prowess can provide a better return.
- You've decided to enroll in a prepaid tuition plan, but you'd also like to save for room and board (which aren't covered by some prepaid tuition plans).
- You want to get the state tax deduction by investing in your state's program, but you don't want all your college savings in the hands of money managers, so you open a Coverdell ESA and make your own investment decisions.

■ Your kids will go to college after 2011, and you don't want to risk Congress not extending the tax-free status of 529 withdrawals. So you put the first $2,000 in a Coverdell ESA and the rest in a 529 plan.

■ You anticipate that your child will attend private elementary school, private secondary school, or both, so you contribute to a Coverdell ESA (since it can be used to save for precollege education costs). Because contributions to a Coverdell ESA are limited to $2,000 a year, you are concerned that the funds in the account will not be enough to pay for elementary, secondary, and postsecondary school, so you contribute to a 529 plan as well.

JUST DO SOMETHING!

Having fun yet? As you deliberate among these options, don't let yourself succumb to analysis paralysis. Saving *something* is much better than delaying while you keep mulling things over. Due to the higher contribution limits and favorable financial-aid treatment, 529 savings plans are the best deals for most people. If your state offers benefits for participating in its 529 plan, and the plan offers at least five investment options that don't charge over 1.25 percent annually, then consider signing up with the home team. If you decide later that it isn't the best plan for you, transfer to another 529 plan.

If you're leaning toward a Coverdell ESA but still have doubts, go ahead and open one. *The funds can be transferred to a 529 plan without penalty.* That's right, you can switch if additional research convinces you that a 529 plan would be better.

However, taking money from a 529 plan and putting it in a Coverdell ESA *will* incur distribution penalties and will *not* escape the $2,000 annual contribution limit.

OFFBEAT BUT WORTH CONSIDERING: UPROMISE

Meandering off the beaten path for a minute or two. . . .

If you're interested in painlessly racking up dollars for your future college scholars, click over to www.upromise.com. It's a program that rewards your patronage of certain businesses with contributions to a college savings plan. Last time we checked, if you purchased a book at Borders or Borders.com, you'd get 2 percent of the purchase price contributed to the college kitty. Sign up for America Online, get $50. The purchase of a box of Kellogg's cereal at your grocery store will get you 5 percent.

Here's how it works: Register with Upromise, submit your credit-card information, and open a tax-advantaged 529 plan for the beneficiary of your choice (e.g., your son, your granddaughter, your niece, yourself). Use your credit card to purchase merchandise from participating companies, or sign up for specific programs (such as AT&T's 4 percent back on long distance service), or shop online through Upromise's website. The rebate is automatically deposited into your account; you don't have to save receipts or submit forms.

Upromise's benefits are hard to find fault with. But keep in mind:

■ Any savings accumulated through Upromise should be seen as a supplement to a college savings plan, not a replacement. Upromise estimates that an average participant can save around $8,000 for college over fifteen years. That's better than a kick in the pants, but not enough to pay for a four-year degree. (Upromise does provide a nifty calculator that estimates how much you can save based on your spending habits.)

■ Don't use the program to justify unnecessary purchases. The $5 you'd get from the 2 percent Toys "R" Us rebate is not reason enough to buy the $200 Xbox starter kit.

■ Read the fine print. If you don't follow the rules, you won't get credit. For example, the Upromise site says that if you use a real estate agent from a selected agency, $1/2$ percent of the sale or purchase price of a home will be contributed to your account. However, you must follow a specific procedure, and residents of certain states are ineligible. And, um, we'd still recommend you try to bargain down the purchase price of that house.

■ Submitting your credit-card number and other personal information will let Upromise and its partners know a lot about you. Make sure you're comfortable with the privacy policy.

To learn more—including which thousands of restaurants and retailers participate—visit www.upromise.com. Used conscientiously, the program can help turn your day-to-day spending into free tuition.

FINANCIAL AID

As you know by now, the type of college savings account you choose will likely affect how much financial aid your student will be offered. So let's get a few things straight about financial aid.

■ When it comes to calculating a student's expected family contribution, income is a bigger factor than assets. It is important to consider how your college savings account might affect aid eligibility, but it's not as important as what shows up on the student's and parents' tax returns.

■ *The vast majority of financial aid comes in the form of student loans.* You may be offered a smaller financial-aid package if you've saved over the years, but that usually just means you'll be offered smaller loans.

■ Who owns the college savings account is important in the calculation of expected family contribution. The federal formula factors in 35 percent of the student's assets, but only 5.6 percent of the parents' assets. If you're looking to increase your chances for a generous aid package, keep assets in the parents' name.

Financial-aid practices change all the time, so check in occasionally with the Department of Education and with prospective schools to monitor policy updates.

AFFORDING COLLEGE AT THE LAST MINUTE

And now the section that you've probably all been waiting for.

Drum roll please, Duke.

It's time for our game of *Trying to make up for past laziness, poverty, ignorance, or indiscretion by saving for college all at once!* It's not going to happen quite that way, but we do have a bit of advice for those in a bind.

First off, even if your pride and joy is nearing the end of high school and you haven't saved a dime, don't give up hope. Junior isn't doomed to a life of flipping burgers. There are several things you can do to improve your situation.

For starters, Junior might delay going to college for one or more years. Working for a bit right out of high school can be a smart move. He and you can save money for college as he works. Both of us agree that we would have appreciated our own college years more had we taken a year off between high school and college to muck about in the (working) world. If we'd been talented computer programmers who took a year off to work at Microsoft, we probably wouldn't have needed college, period, and might've attended years later simply because we wanted to. Trading some $100,000 of undergraduate *expense* for $100,000 of earned *income* and a sweet positioning four years later that would have been well up the totem pole from new college graduates (our peers), well— sorry, just daydreaming. Lost youth. . . .

Also consider having Junior focus on less expensive schools, such as in-state public universities, which tend to charge much lower tuition. Local schools have additional benefits, such as extra scholarship opportunities and reduced travel costs to and from school. (Choose a very local school, and Junior can live at home, saving thousands.) Another option is for Junior to attend a community college in the first year, before transferring to a bigger, more expensive school in his last years. A relatively new possibility is pursuing a degree offered by many schools via the Internet.

These options might not even be necessary. Start looking into scholarships; Junior might qualify for one or more. You don't always have to be a genius to earn them—some are meant for violin-playing Lithuanian-Americans and others for lifeguards with family ties to some association or organization. Some are for students from a particular state who want to study a particular subject. There's a wide range; see our list of resources at chapter's end.

Consider loans. We've barely talked about these, but as long as you don't end up borrowing too much, they are an effective way to finance schooling, often at very attractive interest rates.

Finally, Junior should apply to one or more of his dream schools, because you never know—they might offer a financial-aid package that helps make it all affordable.

CREATIVE ALTERNATIVES

A new education-financing possibility we've just heard of is at www.myrichuncle.com. The company matches investors with college or graduate students. In exchange for school funds, the investors will be due a percentage of the students' income for a set number of years. This might be a win-win deal, if unusual.

Another idea comes to us via our a "Baby Boomer" online discussion board, where Fool Community member Kirakat explained how she paid for law school:

> Another thing that I did was to become "independent" at the end of my junior year of college. I didn't take any money from my folks, paid rent for the six weeks I lived at their house in the summer, and survived on my own earnings. Fortunately, I was a resident assistant at one of the dorms, so room, board, and extra cash were provided for. And a handful of scholarships took care of tuition, fees, and books.
>
> Although my dad complained about losing the tax deduction, since I was on my own for a year before going to law school, only my income counted in determining eligibility for financial assistance. That enabled me to pay for law school without help from my folks. Since I was the oldest of four, I figured it would be easier on them that way. I did take out some loans, but nothing compared to the amounts kids have to take out today, and I was able to pay mine off in six years instead of ten.

I don't know if that scenario would work today, but since my dad's income was always too high for any kind of assistance or loans, it did make a big difference for me.

Fellow Fool Community member Lee points out another workable strategy:

> If you live in state A and your kid wants to go to the public university in state B, have her take a year off and get some sort of job or internship or something that enables her to establish residency in state B. You can still gift her money, but the difference between resident and nonresident tuition is enormous—at least at U.C. Berkeley and Michigan, two I considered. And I did go to grad school at Berkeley—*after* establishing residency.

If your child is establishing residency far from you, it doesn't necessarily mean that he or she needs to live in a ramshackle apartment on the edge of town at the tender age of eighteen. See if a friend or relative in the area will take in your child as a paying boarder. Let's make it clearer: If necessary, up to (but not including) the point of using physical force, compel Uncle Arnie to get off his duff and open up his door over there in New Mexico so that little Freddie can move in with him prior to four sunny years at UNM.

Uncle Arnie could probably use the sunshine himself.

Action Plan

To begin to get your parental ducks in a row, here's a short list of the most important things you should do to prepare for your child's education:

(1) Begin saving and investing now for your children's future needs. Don't put it off.
(2) Learn about your options regarding saving and investment accounts and plans, and choose the ones that make the most sense for you.
(3) Involve your children in financial matters and planning.

Teach them about saving and investing. Get them a copy of *The Motley Fool Investment Guide for Teens*. Get them invested (so to speak) in their future.

(4) Take advantage of the many resources listed below. We didn't have the space to tell you *all* you need to know, so these books and websites will give you more ideas.

Resources

www.campustours.com: Tour colleges, virtually

www.collegeboard.com: Information on college planning and finances

www.ed.gov: The U.S. Department of Education

www.studentaid.ed.gov: A comprehensive resource on student financial aid from the U.S. Department of Education

www.fool.com/college/college.htm: The Fool's own College Savings Center

www.mapping-your-future.org: Information for parents and students on financial strategies, career options, and college planning

www.myrichuncle.com: Get hooked up with someone who will fund your education for a cut of your later income

www.petersons.com: Information on college searches, test preparation, and financial aid

www.savingforcollege.com: A site mentioned earlier, rich in information on 529 plans

Here are some websites where you can look up available scholarships:

www.college-scholarships.com
www.collegescholarships.com
www.fastweb.com
www.finaid.org
www.wiredscholar.com

And loan information is here:

www.estudentloan.com
www.salliemae.com
www.studentloan.com

Some (of many) books on paying for college and the planning process:

The A's and B's of Academic Scholarships, by Anna Leider
The College Admissions Mystique, by Bill Mayher
The Fiske Guide to Getting into the Right College, by Edward B. Fiske and Bruce G. Hammond
Get Into Any College: Secrets of Harvard Students, by Gen S. Tanabe and Kelly Y. Tanabe
The Government Financial Aid Book: The Insider's Guide to State and Federal Government Grants and Loans, by Student Financial Services
How to Go to College Almost for Free, by Ben Kaplan
The Motley Fool's Guide to Paying for School: How to Cover Education Costs from K to PhD, by Robert Brokamp
The Scholarship Book 2003, by National Scholarship Research Service

Chapter Thirteen

Making Your Children Self-Sufficient

Judge me not by what I do, but by what my children achieve.
—ERSKINE BOWLES

IT'S ONE THING to put our children through college. It's another thing—related but different—to give them enough knowledge and confidence and financial savvy so they'll be able to carry on independently after college. Our underlying assumption in this chapter—let us know if we're off base here—is that you'd rather not have to financially carry your offspring over the next few decades. We're assuming that you love your children, that at the core of your being is a desire to see them living joyful lives. But for a multitude of reasons involving everyone's best self-interest, you'd also love to see them enjoying self-sufficient lives. Since they may have received little or no education about money from school, it's up to you to help them most of all.

We're just cockeyed, swaggering, or perhaps addlebrained enough to think we can help. But can we do so engagingly, painlessly, gloriously? Let's hope so. Here are our six simple ways to make your children self-sufficient.

(1) ESTABLISH SOME INCENTIVE FOR FINANCIAL DISCIPLINE

In Thomas Sowell's wonderful book *Basic Economics*, he presents a behavioral economic theory that should startle none of us. Incentives matter. The rabbit seeks the carrot. Bridge players battle for master points. A rat presses a lever for food pellets. The executive goes for his bonus. Employees work harder at the prospect of a raise.

As with other life forms, so, too, with your children. Your children will respond to the incentives you set. Reward them highly for good grades; they will study harder. Withdraw a healthy allowance if their bedrooms aren't spotless and, zing, the rooms are aglow. (We're not saying that this doesn't come with some resistance and bellyaching.) Support them with a smile and an embrace when they fail, and they'll gain resilience in the face of adversity.

Unfortunately, even a cursory awareness of the consumer debt in America today proves that we haven't been placing incentive carrots in the right places. Perhaps because so many of us haven't done so, our children have not been motivated to save enough, let alone invest. Instead, they expect they'll still get all those compact discs without having to set aside savings themselves. They may expect you to help pay down their Neiman Marcus charge card. They expect the car. College tuition. The cash needed for changes in fashion. Free money to come their way from the ATM machine, once you tap a few buttons.

FOR FURTHER THINKING

The late Mister Rogers on attitudes about money:

Feelings about money. You know, saving and spending, holding back and letting go, start very early in our lives. Stingy people have often been forced to give when they were very young, when they weren't ready. Generous people have often been really appreciated when they were very young. I think it is so important to remember that everyone has something to give.

Want to teach your children financial self-sufficiency?

Install an elegant rewards system.

Here's how: Match the savings of your children from their ear-liest years, as far along as you choose to. For every dollar your child commits to save over five years, match it with one or more extra dollars, just as corporations match their employees' 401(k) savings.

What's the right amount? Depends on the child, the parent, the family. One correct answer is "Whatever will cause them to save." For many, that will be a one-for-one match. Other kids might need to be enticed further. Along the way, you can probably alter the plan. Perhaps from ages eight to fifteen, your child gets one dollar for every one she saves. From fifteen to twenty-five your contribu-tion is reduced to 50 cents for every dollar. (Notice this doesn't have to end when she graduates from college.) From ages twenty-five to thirty-five, as her income increases, you lower the match to a more manageable 25 cents for every dollar saved. This can be a lifelong offer—a Great Big Carrot.

Depending on how sophisticated you want to get, you can fur-ther increase your match for every dollar your child commits to investment for ten years or more. As you'll learn in the next sec-tion, teaching your daughters and sons to compound their savings over long periods of time is handing them a ticket to the financial freedom party (the one where partygoers work out of love for a job rather than desperate economic necessity).

A simple matching plan will turn your child not into a rabbit but into a CEO of his or her own financial empire, someone who takes fiscal responsibility for the future, who comes to understand the value of a dollar, who early on learns the benefits of saving, and whom you will not have to support through borrowings against your retirement plan.

(2) CELEBRATE THE POWER OF COMPOUNDING

Incentive plan in place, it's time to teach your children about the power of compounding applied to money. Chances are they haven't learned it yet. High school math classes easily could have helped them master the formula, but the mother lode of mathematical training in this country is designed to prepare children for the Scholastic Aptitude Test. We load them up with theory—high algebra, calculus, and trigonometry—and often forget to teach them all the glorious application (which is completely irrelevant on the SATs).

Don't believe us?

Why else would generations of young math students labor through inane problems that pit train A in Chicago against train B in Philadelphia? Because we've been taught math *theory,* often without any useful applications. We fill their heads with memorized equations, set them up to master entrance exams, then send them off to college. Once there, they borrow money at 18 percent interest on credit cards (remarkably poor application of all that mathematical theory, eh?). Then they spend their twenties trying to figure their way out of minimum monthly payments on that debt. After marriage, the births of their children set them back further. It isn't until their forties that they've battled their way out of high-interest debt. And then they're expected to pay for their kids to attend college. They'll have to take some drastic steps to retire at sixty-five.

Why all that? In part because they never had math theory applied to basic finance. Did they learn about compounding back in seventh grade? No, they were multiplying fractions. Was it reinforced in tenth grade? No, they were calculating the volume of spheres. Did their university struggle to reteach the formula during freshman year? Of course not. (In fact, many universities derive revenue from selling the financial information of their incoming students to the credit-card companies! Gasp.) Was there a brushup on math as applied to money when they arrived at graduate school? Certainly not.

The only way you can guarantee that your children will understand compound growth as applied to money—which should be their primary source of monetary wealth—is if *you* teach them. Teach your children, whatever their age, the wondrous power of geometric growth. It's the equation that Einstein called a miracle. It will turn $1,000—invested in the stock market at the birth of your daughter—into $1 million in her retirement. It has made eventual millionaires out of young paupers.

What is compound growth?

Let's compare it first to its cousin, linear growth. Think of your salary. Each year you're paid, say, $60,000 for the work you do. If you see no cost-of-living increases or performance bonuses for a decade, you'll generate $600,000 of salary income. That's linear growth of capital. Each year you earn the same $60,000 for your yearlong effort.

Compound growth of capital is quite different. Your money grows in percentage terms. Historically, the United States stock market has compounded 11 percent annual returns for investors. Let's say you start with $60,000. In ten years, through stock market compounding of 11 percent per year, it will grow to around $170,000.

Now let's compare the two.

With *linear* growth of $60,000 a year in salary money, you end up with $600,000. With *compound* growth of $60,000 in investment money, you end up with $170,000. Over the ten-year period, linear growth far surpasses compound growth. And that, mon Fool, is precisely why so many young professionals don't invest early on. Through divine intuition or back-of-the-envelope math, they calculate that they'll make far more in the short term from salary than from an investment portfolio. So, then, investing's not worth it. They have the right answer to that question, but they've asked the wrong question.

What if, instead, they played the scenario out over a forty-year period? The $60,000 annual salary would then add up to $2.4 million in take-home pay. There's the linear growth. What of the $60,000 in onetime investment money, earning 11 percent per year? $3.9 million. Taken forward another ten years, the salary money grows to $3 million. The investment money grows to $11.1 million. And which, we ask, demands more labor? Going to work every weekday for fifty years or investing once up front and earning no more than the stock market's average rate of return?

Let's run one more comparison of linear growth versus compound growth. Refer to our suggestion that $1,000 invested in common stocks for a newborn will blossom into $1 million in her retirement. That's the power of compound growth over a long period of time. Here's how that happens. Start with $1,000 and see it expand through the years:

1. $1,110	16. $5,311	31. $25,410	46. $121,579	61. $581,704
2. $1,232	17. $5,895	32. $28,206	47. $134,952	62. $645,691
3. $1,368	18. $6,544	33. $31,308	48. $149,797	63. $716,717
4. $1,518	19. $7,263	34. $34,752	49. $166,275	64. $795,556
5. $1,685	20. $8,062	35. $38,575	50. $184,565	65. $883,067
6. $1,870	21. $8,949	36. $42,818	51. $204,867	66. $980,204
7. $2,076	22. $9,934	37. $47,528	52. $227,402	67. $1,088,027
8. $2,305	23. $11,026	38. $52,756	53. $252,417	
9. $2,558	24. $12,239	39. $58,559	54. $280,182	
10. $2,839	25. $13,585	40. $65,001	55. $311,002	
11. $3,152	26. $15,080	41. $72,151	56. $345,213	
12. $3,498	27. $16,739	42. $80,088	57. $383,186	
13. $3,883	28. $18,580	43. $88,897	58. $425,337	
14. $4,310	29. $20,624	44. $98,676	59. $427,124	
15. $4,785	30. $22,892	45. $109,530	60. $524,057	

No doubt, you immediately note how relatively little money is made in the first ten years. In fact, after twenty years, the $1,000 investment has earned as much as the investment individually in the forty-fifth year. This is the power of compounding at work. Time makes the money.

What's particularly interesting about this table is that you can go directly to your age and see how much you would have to put in now, at the market's average return, to have a million dollars by age sixty-seven. For a newborn, it took only $1,000. By fifteen, you needed to invest $4,800 for fifty-two years. By age forty, it would take $65,000. And if you waited until fifty, it would take $185,000 to have a million at sixty-seven.

This is the power and glory and beauty of compounding applied to money. A thousand dollars invested at your son's birth is earning him over $60,000 a year in his sixties. The three key variables behind compound interest are: (1) the time horizon for the investment; (2) the average annual rate of return; and (3) the size of the initial investment.

Ah, but—blessed good news for all of us—enter one additional factor. If you've spent the last few minutes weeping into the tables, wishing your high school had taught you this, it's time to heed a magical fourth variable: *frequency of investment.* How often you add money substantially alters how well you do. If you're fifty-three years old, recognize that you may well live another four decades. At least two of those decades should include some good solid saving, investment, and compound growth. If the market matches its historical average over the next twenty-five years, you'll have made eight times your initial investment. And you'll have made seven, six, five, four, three, and two times the monies you added along the way.

But hold on a sec!

This section isn't about compounding and *you . . .*

We've been talking about making your *children* self-sufficient. And you've taken two fine steps already: (1) created a savings and investment incentive for your children; and (2) taught them the power of compounded growth (just show them the table on the previous page).

FOR FURTHER THINKING

**Today *show weatherman Al Roker on his experience
with money growing up:***

Al Roker: I got an allowance, and I was made to save half of it. I had to put half of it in a savings account. Same with when I started working after school. My parents were frugal.
David: So at what age did this allowance begin for you? It sounds like it is something that went on for years.
Roker: Yeah, it just stopped last year. *(Laughter)* They finally cut me off at $30 a week. Said, "That is enough. You are going to work on your own. We don't think you need the allowance anymore."
Tom: I think I remember you telling us during your first book that you got a surprise later on. Some of that money came back.
Roker: Yeah, Mom and Dad actually had been saving some of my allowance for me all the way through, and they gave it back.

---

(3) SHOW THEM HOW COMPOUNDING CAN
CLOBBER THEM

Compounding would not be such a tsunami if it didn't have both the power to build and the power to break. The most awesome mathematical formulae can create and destroy with equal fury. Compounding rapidly forms and multiplies the cells—from zero to a zillion—that are a newborn child. Compounding also speedily forms cancerous cells that swiftly destroy human life. Creation and cancer . . . apply these concepts to money, and you've grasped the next two steps.

The cancer in personal finance is the credit card. The average college graduate carries over $2,000 of credit-card debt at 15 percent interest. The average American household is weighted down with over $8,000 of credit-card debt. Need we explain to you, Jedi Fool, the allure of convenient short-term credit? Let's assume not. However, we can assume that your average college graduate is only beginning to learn about the agony of interest rates.

The $2,000 of credit-card debt on the back of the young college student is working through its own compounding. If the bills went unpaid, the 15 percent interest rate would introduce the following pain over the next ten years.

Year 1. $2,300
2. $2,645
3. $3,042
4. $3,498
5. $4,023
6. $4,626
7. $5,320
8. $6,118
9. $7,036
10. $8,091

As you know, credit-card companies don't let their compounding bills go unpaid. If they did, supported by tightening bankruptcy laws, they would own America many times over within two generations.

Never mind, though. Just look at that tenth year: $8,091. Now recall: The average American household carries over $8,000 of credit-card debt at 15 percent interest. The accumulation of debt in our compounding example gets you right there in ten years. In other words, what credit-card companies are saying is that they would let the average college graduate let their debts go without payment for ten years (actually, far longer, since some households carry as much as $50,000 in credit-card debt).

What are you to do to help your future generations of little Fools avoid this perilous path? Here's one thing: Establish a small incentive—somewhere between $20 and $40 per month—for the prompt repayment of all credit-card debt. Extend the incentive from ages twenty to thirty. If your child nails every month, you'll end up paying between $2,400 and $4,800 over the full decade. Sound like a lot? It's nothing compared to some of the postoperative bailouts we've read about at Fool.com. If that is too much for you to afford right now, set it lower—$5 or $10 a month to remind your children not to fall down this hole.

Call it a preemptive incentive. Such devices can set up your children for success during the most tenuous years of their financial lives, in which a few good or bad decisions can dramatically affect their fortunes as adults. Remember, if they wind up having to service 15 percent interest rates on their debt, why would they ever simultaneously invest in the stock market and its 10 to 11 percent earnings per year? Those with double-digit-rated credit-card debt err if they invest money in anything except repayment. Keeping your kids out of this from the get-go means freeing them to be savers, not debtors.

(4) INTRODUCE THEM TO THE TOTAL STOCK MARKET INDEX FUND

Time to flip the coin from tails (credit-card debt) to heads, which is the Total Stock Market Index Fund. Where credit-card debt enslaves, quiet and low-fee long-term market returns will liberate.

You're familiar with this fund (offered most effectively and least expensively by the Vanguard family of mutual funds in Pennsylvania). We consider it the go-to option for so many people in so many situations, united by two common characteristics: They have time to leave the money invested but don't have time to do their own research. Enter this, the most easily understood mutual fund in the land. Out of the nine thousand or so public companies in America, this mutual fund buys shares in all that exceed a minimum size, meaning almost *four thousand* of them. The net result is performance that near perfectly approximates the returns of the entire U.S. stock market.

Teach your kids about this fund and its five magical elements.

First, because it purchases shares in almost four thousand different companies, it provides investors with total diversification in common stocks. No reliance on IBM to perform well over the next five years. No hoping against hope that Kmart turns its business around. No getting down on your hands and knees and pleading with the almighty to endow Lucent's executives with the creativity, integrity, and dexterity to bring the business back from the dead. The Total Stock Market Index Fund spreads your risk by providing you ownership in virtually every public American business you can name. It's the perfect ballast to your child's long-term portfolio of investments.

Second, you know what you own! Your child will not wake up to a phone call from his broker, apologizing for speculating in coffee-bean futures. Your child will not own a mutual fund whose manager buys all the hot stocks at the end of each quarter in order to list them in the fund's performance report. Your child will not wake past midnight with desperate fears that the cattle-farming and Hollywood-film limited partnerships that her third cousin Bob got her into (a pox on whoever it was that sat her next to him last Thanksgiving) will go kaput (by the way, they probably will). Instead, your child will own the entire U.S. market. Signed, sealed, delivered.

Third, teach him that the fees tied to this fund are the lowest in the industry. Because the mutual fund's buying is automated— "Computer, go out and buy shares of these 3,739 companies"— you will not be overpaying for stock analysts, board meetings in Bermuda, three hundred sources of equity research, and the heavy trading associated with most stock funds today. The annual cost of Vanguard's fund is 0.20 percent. The annual cost for the average equity mutual fund in America is about 1.25 percent, six times higher per year. In a universe where the market rises 10 to 11 percent per average year, that 1 percentage point difference compounded over time is *huge,* and it helps explain why index funds beat managed mutual funds so frequently. Low fees mixed with outperformance—your children deserve it.

Fourth, one word: taxes. The average mutual fund in America over the past five years has traded into and out of practically all hundred or so of its holdings each year. That overactive trading delivers high short-term capital-gains taxes to your doorstep each April 15. If mutual funds were required to estimate and clearly disclose their after-tax returns, their shareholders would faintingly grab a rail. The Total Stock Market Index Fund does very little trading, most of it mechanical, as money flows in and out of the fund. It generally buys and holds its positions. That makes it among the most tax-efficient stock-market investments in the world. Paying taxes each year on your investments is a massive interruption to the process of compounding—a process your child understands thoroughly now, right? Thanks to you.

Fifth, because the fund is designed to match the market's returns, you can reasonably estimate how it will do over twenty-year periods. Jeremy Siegel's fine book *Stocks for the Long Run* presents stock-performance data going back to 1800. The resilience and brilliance of the U.S. stock market is very much in evidence. Every which way you slice the performance numbers, the stock market generates a steady 8 to 12 percent per year over the long term. Your child should be investing in twenty-year bunches. Given the probabilities, you can estimate what invested dollars will be worth ten, twenty, and fifty years from now. You can show them the table in Step Three and point to their rewards.

For us, the Total Stock Market Index Fund from Vanguard provides a simple, sturdy, elegant backbone to the portfolio of any long-term investor in stocks. Frankly, we'd love a plucky competitor to come along and improve on Vanguard's model; we have no interest in being shills for this fund. As of yet, that hasn't happened. This is your best, most diversified, least expensive, most tax-efficient, most predictable alternative in stocks for your children.

(5) EMPHASIZE SMALL, REGULAR SAVINGS

Home again, home again, home again, run. We're nearing the finish line to creating economic self-sufficiency among your children. What kind of world would we live in if parents knew to teach these half-dozen simple lessons to their offspring? If the majority of baby boomers had learned this in school, they would now be driving toward second careers, a flow of hobbies, traveling the world over, with a chicken in every pot. Or something like that. Let's hope we get it right with this generation.

Step five is simple. No need for intellectual aerobics. Just persuade the young people in your life to set aside $10 here and $50 there for long-term investment. The grown Fools whose parents convinced them to save and invest 10 percent of any incoming money, automatically, are happy. They're the grown Fools with the second career, the hobbies, the world travel, and that chicken on every platter. It's a priceless tip: Save 10 percent of any money you get, right off. Drop it over into the Total Stock Market Index Fund. Watch it grow. Make it sing. Dance a jig around it. Throw confetti. Pour champagne. Smile the while away, with rose petals flung down the crystal stairs of your life.

Your children will be self-sufficient if they pay down credit-card debt instantly, save 10 percent of any money they get, dump it into the Total Market Index Fund, and then simply master step six.

(6) TEACH THEM TO DO WHAT THEY LOVE

This is as valuable as the five previous steps combined. You can have all the money in the world. You can sleep in diamonds and dine on caviar. Your servants can oil your feet, comb your hair, drop grapes in your mouth, renew your license at the Department of Motor Vehicles, and throw clean silk sheets on the bed every night. Your life can heave with sinful luxury. But it will be unhappy, often terribly so, if you do not know—and do not do—what you love.

If you thoroughly love what you do and bring joy to those around you, then you'll need very little capital to satisfy you. It'll

SETTING UP A ROTH IRA FOR YOUR CHILDREN

A Foolish Tip from Motley Fool Community Member Cathy Giunta

You can set up a Roth IRA for your child at any age. The only requirement is that they earn the money and get paid at a rate that anyone doing the job would make. For instance, if your child baby-sits, washes cars, mows lawns, sells lemonade, or paints houses, he and you could put any of that money into a Roth IRA. My kids, who just turned twelve, have been pet-sitting in the neighborhood when people are gone. They get $10 a day, which they split. Around here, professional pet-sitters get $13 a visit, so their income is in the ballpark.

I set up Roth IRAs for my children because my father taught me that you can never start to plan your retirement too early. At this age, my kids get an allowance and have few needs and expenses. They understand about investing and how compounding works. In fact, they already have brokerage accounts that they use to invest in stocks we choose together. The Roth IRA was simply an extension of the financial plan I'm trying to help them build. Anything they can put in now will have thirty to forty years of compounding, and that's if they want to retire early. So we sat down, and I actually did the math with them on what $100 would be if it grew at 8 percent for the next thirty years, and that worked out to $1,000, so that's ten times what they started with. Imagine that with larger amounts, as they get older and start to have steady jobs in the summer and after school—it could be a substantial sum when they are older. As they learn these lessons now, I go a long way toward ensuring their financial health throughout their lives.

Here's how I helped them set it up.

Once the children have earned income, it's easy. We just went down to the credit union where we have their savings accounts and opened a Roth IRA. Fill out the forms with the initial deposit, and it's done. You can start small, then move the Roth IRA to a brokerage account for investments in index funds or stocks after they have accumulated a few hundred dollars. They will not be able to withdraw this money until they're sixty, so they'll have many decades of compounding. (If they want an account from which they can withdraw money along the way, research custodial accounts.)

Before closing out this sidebar, I wanted to say I never would have started all this if it weren't for my father teaching me about money as a child. I strongly agree with my dad. It's never too early to start planning and saving for retirement. In the case of my children, it is not unimaginable that they could have enough saved by the time they are forty to retire, if they so choose. And as I like to tell them, life is all about choices . . . being able to have plenty of choices at each stage of your life.

take only a basic financial plan and the simple discipline of living within your means to ensure happiness. We've said as much in many of the speeches we've given across the country over the past decade. We do not believe success guarantees happiness. Conversely, we've never met a happy person whom we did not consider successful.

Teach your children to search out their loves in life. Gird that enthusiasm with five simple lessons about money. What will come of it? Not just self-sufficient children. Far more. Self-sufficient, happy children, and parents with peace of mind.

Action Plan

■ Get your kids saving. Teach them to put aside a portion of every dollar they get their hands on.

■ Get your children investing. You might start with one or two shares of familiar companies (PepsiCo, Microsoft, Kellogg, Nike, McDonald's, Wal-Mart, etc.) when they're young, then help them follow the progress of their companies. As they become teens, they can begin investing more significant amounts regularly, perhaps in an index fund or some carefully selected stocks.

■ Get your kids to be smart about money and how they spend it. Teach them about the dangers of credit-card debt and the futility of lotteries. Help them learn to comparison-shop and think twice or more before making any major purchase.

■ Involve your children in your family's financial matters and planning. They should understand utility bills, for example, and how they can help minimize them.

■ Help your kids become financially savvy by pointing them to our online nook for teens, at www.fool.com/teens. Or get them a copy of our book, *The Motley Fool Investment Guide for Teens*. Get your young ones "invested" in their future.

Chapter Fourteen

Planning Your Estate

There's no reason to be the richest man in the cemetery. You can't do any business from there.

—Colonel Sanders

 A LOT OF BOOKS about financial planning will give you the same basically tired advice about how you should, you *really should*, make a will or a trust.

Yawn.

This is conventional wisdom at its quintessence.

You haven't bought that sort of book, have you? We think planning for how your money is handled after your death is extremely overrated. You're going to be *dead*, aren't you? We all will one fateful day. So why the heck should any of us want to waste our precious few moments on earth planning for how our silly assets are going to be redistributed to a silly world in which we will have no role to play?

Indeed, your money will do just as well going to the government and meeting the needs of all people (including government bureaucrats) rather than just a few loved ones whom you have privileged with your stuff. That would seem fairer, right?

No?

You mean you actually *do* care about those close to you and how they get on, even if you're not around? You say it matters to you, the degree of comfort and convenience and happiness that you create—or fail to create—for loved ones by planning where your assets will go after you do? You say you think this is partly about respecting other people's time? That no matter how large or small your pile of worldly possessions, your own legacy counts, you wish to be well thought of?

In that case . . .

Perhaps we should come clean and let you know that we entirely agree. We began this chapter sarcastically, urging you to recall that sarcasm be the wit of Fools. Yep, the previous statement was a desperate ploy to engage you on this topic, particularly since so many people practically insist on *avoiding* thoughts about their own death.

So let's close our section on "Having More Than Enough" with what to many people seems a more-than-enough thing to do: to plan your estate, to make a will. We suspect that if there were more self-interest in all this, humans would be more diligent about setting up estates for our heirs. However, the stark truth is that we will not be using our finances after our deaths. Beyond some good words in the Bible about stewardship, we're not aware of any Christian teachings—or any other religious teachings, for that matter—that suggest God won't like it if you don't write a will. So absent clear personal gain or anything like a divine threat, the act of writing one will probably remain an altruistic, unpopular act.

So let's get altruistic, shall we?

WHAT WE'RE GOING TO ACCOMPLISH HERE

It would take thousands of pages to provide encyclopedic estate-planning advice applicable to every reader. This is a very individual process, much better accomplished by sitting down with a respectable lawyer to figure out what you have and how you uniquely wish to distribute what is yours. We can't do that for you in the pages of this book, but what we *can* do is:

(1) Make it clear that you should take care of this task, preferably in the next few months (don't put it off!)—the primary drive behind this chapter.

(2) Help you locate a good estate planner, as opposed to a medi-ocre one or one who is downright harmfully bad.

(3) Provide you some of the basics that will have you thinking smart and Foolishly as you prepare to go through this important process.

Much of the material here is applicable and useful for you as an heir. It's very helpful to understand something about how your parents' or others' money is set up to come to you, since you'll make better decisions with more information. So this chapter isn't just about pitching your assets to others; it's also something of a catcher's mitt for you, the heir.

With all that said, let's shift to a few tips for finding a good estate planner.

CHOOSING THE RIGHT ESTATE-PLANNING LAWYER

Perhaps your single best option for good references comes from your local county or state bar association. Philadelphia lawyer and Motley Fool member Mark points out that accomplished and knowledgeable lawyers are the ones generally invited to give bar seminars to other lawyers on your topic of concern. Call up the association, ask for the continuing legal education (CLE) depart-ment, and find out which local lawyers are lecturing on estates and wills.

A fine second option is to call your bank's trust department (as-suming it has one) and ask the trust officer for a good recommen-dation. Trust officers frequently work with lawyers specializing in estate planning, and any trust officer worth his or her salt should have one or more solid references for you.

If not, hey, consider switching banks!

Moving down the totem pole, a third option is your own net-work of friends and family. If you hear a convincing testimonial about an estate planner from your brother-in-law or your invest-ment-banker college chum, you're usually on to a pretty good thing. However, be aware that it's difficult for a lay person to adequately and accurately rate the work of an estate attorney, which is why we put this option third. If you go the friends-and-family route, try to corroborate any testimonials with similarly supportive words from a few others, preferably including a lawyer.

Assuming that one of these approaches has identified one or more decent candidates, here are a few more considerations.

First, insist on using an attorney who *specializes* in trusts and estates law. While a general practitioner can prepare a simple will, most wills are not simple. This area of the law is among the most dynamic, with its ever-changing legal landscape and tax implications. Trust your trust attorney. Work with a specialist.

Second, remember that you should probably be reviewing your documents every five years or so. If you switch estate planners or firms, you'll frequently get the advice that "your old documents are outdated and prepared outside our firm—let's just write you up new documents." You may even encounter outright refusals to review others' past work. But new documents are an unnecessary expense, making you a more profitable client than you otherwise should be.

For this reason, select a specialist whose employment and dedication to the field will outlive you. That means inevitably favoring younger planners. Another acceptable option is a planner who is connected to a larger and long-standing firm. You want to know that the firm will still be there should that person move on. You'll minimize avoidable "friction costs" caused by working with more than one planner or firm. The more time you have ahead of you, the more likely this is to occur, and the choosier you should be.

Third, tend to notice whether or not your phone calls of inquiry to a prospective planner are promptly returned. Vicki, a Motley Fool member, considers this perhaps the most important criteria for choosing a lawyer. "After you die, your executor, children, and other heirs will have enough other problems to deal with—getting the lawyer to call them back shouldn't be [one of them]." Prompt callbacks are a great indicator of how efficient and trustworthy any lawyer will wind up being.

Of course, many will rightly argue that what you want most of all in your lawyer is *competence*. That should *never* be assumed. Which is why solid recommendations count.

Now we want to provide you some additional pointers and considerations that should help you work with your estate planner. Most of these mini-sections are relevant to most people and will help you enter your estate planner's office already conversant on some of the topics you'll work through together.

THE BASICS: THE MOST BASIC BASIC

Ahead of time, you should make a plan. It doesn't have to be an elaborate plan. It needn't involve polishing all your brass, learning to hang glide, or tipping off guards at Checkpoint Charlie. Determine upon one or several heirs, get out a fresh sheet of paper, and write down a few sentences about how you will leave your possessions to those named. Who's going to execute your estate for you; will you be naming a trustee (we'll get into this), and if so, who is it; and have you chosen a guardian for your children? It takes five minutes.

So simple, really. It's sad to think that millions upon millions of Americans depart this world intestate—without a valid will, as the lingo goes. They leave their families in a bind, they tie up the courts, and they pays the law-yuhs. We won't be any more dogmatic than that, and we won't bemoan this further. However, we insist that you, dear reader, are not among them.

So now you know the most basic basic. Just make a simple plan.

Oh, and on a side note, the better you prepare yourself by thinking things through in this manner, the cheaper your eventual fees will be. Where time equals money, coming in well prepared is money, no? Bring an updated list of your assets, including details of your life insurance, retirement plans, real estate, and business interests.

THE BASICS: SIMPLE LIST OF
YOUR IMPORTANT PAPERS

The most basic basic may have misled you, since things are not quite that basic. Making a plan for your will (or trust, as we'll consider below) is important, but as you sit down with your estate planner, you should be working toward crafting several important papers in your dossier:

(1) **Your will (last will and testament)**

What is it: Your will details exactly what happens to your property (and potentially your minor dependents) when you die. This is the primary piece of your estate planning.

Where to get it: We've already emphasized the importance of working with an attorney. It won't cost you much, and you'll get the will done quickly and correctly. If you opt for preprinted, fill-in-the-blanks forms and software (which we generally consider a mistake), be sure they are up to date and conform to the laws of your state.

(2) **Living will (advance medical directive)**

What is it: Kind of a silly name, but it says you want the right to die a natural death, free of all costly, extraordinary efforts to keep you alive when your life can be sustained only by artificial means.

Where to get it: This document is available free at virtually every hospital in the nation.

(3) **Durable power of attorney and medical power of attorney (health-care proxy)**

What is it: These documents allow a person of your choice to make decisions on your behalf—financial and legal in the first case, medical in the second—when you are incapacitated.

Where to get it: We suggest you see an attorney for these, too.

Speaking to that last for a sec, forget about death. The odds are quite high that anyone forty-five and over today will reach a temporary period in which he or she is unable to make personal decisions. We're about to provide some real numbers, but we'll make one up here to undergird this point. Here it is: 64.9 percent of all people 45 and over today will be meaningfully incapacitated over the next 35 years, unrelated to terminal illness. In fact, this number cannot be known (though we see estimates like this from time to time). What is important is not the actual number but making it clear that *this is a distinct possibility.* Fortunately, it's one that you can rob of its sting right now by taking the right steps.

THE BASICS: COMMUNICATE WITH THOSE IN YOUR WILL!

Talk to those whom you stipulate in any of these documents. Tell them your wishes. Ask them if they would be willing to make some hard choices if needed. We're tempted to remind you to look 'em in the eye as you ask this question, but we figure you already know that.

THE BASICS: ONE MILLION DOLLARS, AND OTHER REAL NUMBERS TO KNOW

We've emphasized that if you have significant (to you) assets to pass on, you should be working with a good estate planner.

When we speak of "significant" assets, there is one key number that those with larger estates need to know: *one million bucks.* We can separate the world of all estates—that is, the sum total of value left by the deceased (or decedent)—into two classes: those that are taxable and those that are not.

If the decedent's estate is under $1 million, it is exempt from the "death tax." If the decedent's estate is $1 million or more, the dollars beyond the initial $1 million *are* taxable. And that's for those who departed this fair earth in 2003. As you'll see below, the exemption cutoff ratchets up over time. Here's the present table:

Year of Death	Exemption Amount
2003	$1,000,000
2004	$1,500,000
2005	$1,500,000
2006	$2,000,000
2007	$2,000,000
2008	$2,000,000
2009	$3,500,000
2010	Repealed

As you can see, increasing amounts of money will escape tax over the next decade, right up until estate taxes might possibly be repealed in the year 2010. Whether that will come to pass is completely speculative, dependent as it is on the whims of the legislative and executive branches of our government between now and then.

Some more good news: The maximum tax rate on taxable estates similarly declines over time. Take a look.

YEAR OF DEATH	MAXIMUM TAX RATE
2003	49%
2004	48%
2005	47%
2006	46%
2007	45%
2008	45%
2009	45%

Again, nothing is listed for 2010; we'll see if 0 percent winds up being the case. If so, it's definitely worth your while to live past 2009! Back on the exercise bike. . . .

THE BASICS: WILL OR TRUST?

While the decision is not mutually exclusive, you'll want to decide between writing a will or setting up a trust. Documents of the state, wills are filed at court; everything written and determined by a will is part of the public record, available for anyone to see and know. They are often much simpler, and well done, they provide a decisive finality. They can be quick to write, executed one rainy afternoon by the executors, then everyone moves their separate ways. Forever.

Besides their relative simplicity and speed, wills mean that you have a judge who is controlling the process, providing more balanced and objective input and making it easy to resolve any disputes among heirs.

That said, the costs involved with executing a will (probate attorneys and any assigned executors, court fees, etc.) often run much higher than they would for a comparably sized estate made into a trust.

Time is another factor that typically works against wills. Probate court itself takes a minimum of six months but can and often will take a year or more. To generalize, it usually takes several months longer to probate an estate than to administer a trust.

Turning to trusts: They are by contrast private. No one gets to see the details of a private trust except those directly involved. They require a trustee to administer the trust, and they can last a long time, if not into perpetuity—they do in effect allow one to control assets beyond the grave. Also, because they are more thought through, they are more expensive up front. Wills and estates lawyers frequently recommend trusts—often very good advice, but keep in mind that they stand to make a prettier penny from you setting up a trust (which is not to discourage you from doing so, but we at The Motley Fool have always been careful to emphasize how different professionals get paid, because it's very helpful for you to know their carrots).

Because they are more involved, more thought through, and often tighter documents, trusts are also harder to contest than wills. The more money you have, the more worthwhile it is to use a trust. Good estate planners may recommend, for instance, things like AB bypass trusts, which effectively double the $1 million exemption for married couples. If you create an irrevocable life-insurance trust, you can keep your life insurance out of the calculation for the sum total of your estate. Trusts come in many, many flavors.

Your decision to go with a trust or a will (or both) remains *your unique decision,* informed by advice pertinent to your situation provided by your estate planner.

THE BASICS: STEPPED-UP COST BASES

One traditional rule of note both for those leaving assets and for those inheriting them is the stepped-up cost basis that will be applied to many of the assets in an estate; except, typically, tax-deferred accounts like pension plans, IRAs, and annuities.

Inherited property is valued at the date of death or, alternatively, six months after death (whichever is most advantageous). This means that for any assets an heir wishes to sell, there will be virtually no additional tax (beyond any estate tax taken out prior to the assets' distribution).

What's the practical takeaway point? Well, if your father purchased GE stock in 1932 and you just inherited it, you won't have to pay any ungodly large capital-gains tax should you decide to sell. Nope, that GE stock will have its cost basis set at the recent price the stock was trading at. What this means is that you should feel free to sell a lot of these investments (or assets—since, for instance, inherited real estate works the same way), redeploying the money where you find it most relevant and helpful.

Many of us have the goal of simplicity in our financial lives, and the attendant goal of achieving reasonably good returns. Both of these goals, we wish strongly to emphasize, are often well served when you cash out of inherited investments at this advantageous, virtually tax-free time. That's because you then have the *choice* to do what you want with the money, based on the dollars and sense of it (pun intended). Cash out and redeploy.

On our NPR Motley Fool radio show, we talked to a guy who had inherited something like eight different DRP (direct-purchase plan) stocks, three or four shares each, mostly utilities. He was asking about his plan to divert his future savings toward those holdings, continuing to build them up over the course of time. Our advice to him was not to do this. We asked, "What would you do with a thousand dollars—how would you invest it?—if we gave it to you right now?" He didn't have a ready answer; he suggested that maybe he'd put some in an index fund. Please note that he specifically did *not* say, "I would purchase shares of these eight utilities." As you probably surmise, we thought the index fund made a lot more sense for him than adding to stocks that he didn't follow or know much about. Indeed, these stocks were chosen largely because the older woman from whom he received them needed safety and dividends.

Many of us get locked in to this mentality: "That's the way the money was invested, so I guess I should stick with that, or even add to it." We don't think so. The opportunity to sell quickly and tax-efficiently right after an estate is settled is an excellent opportunity to redistribute assets in ways that work for you, that you have a direct connection to, investments that are *yours,* not someone else's.

In these situations, make sure the attorney or trustee provides you with clear documentation as to the cost basis of any asset you inherit, as that will become *your* cost basis if and when you decide to sell.

THE BASICS: HAVING YOUR PAPERS AND BEING ORGANIZED

Speaking of documentation, we must insert a word on the importance of providing good documentation not just with regard to your own estate but *about that documentation.*

You want your stuff to go to the people you love—and you want to leave a lasting memory as the thoughtful, organized, and efficient relative that you are (just don't let anyone open that closet in the front hallway). The surest way to realize your wishes is to simplify your important-paper trail so your family can effortlessly follow it at a time when they are probably thinking of other things.

Motley Fool member John Parsons told us about his mother-in-law's great final gift to the family: "Her estate was an executor's dream." And he wasn't talking about her up-to-date will and power-of-attorney documents.

Nope, her most thoughtful gift to her family was documented on a 50-cent school scribbler. In her neat handwriting, this woman carefully recorded the locations of her safe-deposit box keys, the address of her bank, the address and phone number of her lawyer, the details about her bank accounts, insurance policies, credit cards, and more. There in her own writing was a record of every investment she had ever owned, with the dollar amounts and relevant dates. "She'd even made a couple of comments in random spots in her scribbler from which we deduced that she wanted 'Rock of Ages' played at her funeral," John says.

Though her children—who were named as executors—had never looked at the notebook before, they both knew it existed and had been told numerous times by their mother where to find it. John raises an important point. All the organization in the world doesn't mean diddly unless you *tell your relatives where to find your list of important papers.*

THE BASICS: WHAT TO DO WITH IRAS, 401(K)S, ETC.

Upon your death, the death of an ancestor, or anyone's death, estates are counted up to a total sum. This sum includes any funds remaining in (never drawn down from) tax-deferred retirement accounts. If the estate comes to greater than the $1-plus million exemption, the executor is responsible for paying the necessary estate tax. But when the remaining assets are distributed, there is a distinct difference between how assets *outside* of tax-deferred accounts are treated versus those *within* tax-deferred accounts, the focus of this mini-section.

For tax-deferred accounts, *it is greatly to the advantage of the inheritor to keep the money within the tax shelter.* That's because any inherited money within a 401(k), etc., that is withdrawn becomes taxable as ordinary income. Thus, you want to keep as much as possible within the tax-deferred account.

For situations in which one spouse dies and the other survives, retirement-account assets may be rolled into the living spouse's IRA. For all other situations, we suggest you have the inherited IRA transferred to you as the designated beneficiary. The designated-beneficiary account title would read something like "IRA of mother, deceased, for the benefit of [insert your name here]."

So what does this require? It requires that anyone planning his estate *clearly* designate a beneficiary for every such tax-deferred account. (In some states, you can do this for any and all accounts, bypassing the delay of probate court.) In fact, your will, trust, and other estate-planning documents will *not* override a beneficiary designation for your employee benefits, retirement accounts, or life insurance. Even if you believe you need only a simple will, review your beneficiary designations to make sure they match your intended estate plan. If you have a variety of benefit packages, retirement plans, and insurance policies, you must be careful to confirm that *each* beneficiary designation is correct.

Now, every year after the estate is settled and distributed, beneficiaries of such accounts must take minimum required distributions (MRD, to stuffy estate-planning types or authors looking to save on word counts). The primary goal for anyone who doesn't need all the money as quickly as possible is to minimize their MRD, the amount withdrawn. Why? Because the more you keep tax-deferred for long periods, the more you'll see down the road. What you do withdraw is taxed at your normal income rate, and you must remember to withdraw at least the minimum required, or a nasty 50 percent tax penalty applies to the amount of money you should have withdrawn.

Your accountant or estate planner can help you with the applicable MRD—which is based on your age—but you can get your hands dirty with it now by pointing your Web browser at this IRS website: http://www.irs.gov/pub/irs-pdf/p590supp.pdf.

The IRA or other tax-deferred account will remain there, distributed over life expectancy, dependent on how life expectancy is calculated. Such are the basics of inheriting an IRA, mainly from the point of view of someone inheriting it, though the information is useful when you draw up your estate plans as well.

FINAL BASICS: DIFFERENT STATES, DIFFERENT RESULTS

One size does not fit all when it comes to estate planning. Not only are your assets and wishes different from the next person's, but every state in the union has its own approach to taxes and rules. Even if we provided specific guidance, some ornery state would up and change its rules. That's why the final basic is for you to realize that what you can do in one state, you cannot necessarily do in another.

Probate in California, for instance, ain't traditionally a very pretty picture.

Thomas Jefferson's vision of an America where state and local governments provide a multitude of choices for her citizenry is definitely alive and well when it comes to estate planning. Different states, different results. One size definitely does not fit all.

These examples provide yet another reason to work with an estate-planning professional rather than the software program your niece downloaded off the Internet for you.

Not that you were leaning that way.

FINAL ADMONITION:
IF YOU DON'T DO ANYTHING . . .

If you don't do *anything*—can you say "probate court"?

We knew you could. But why would you want to?

FOR FURTHER THINKING

Elvis Presley Enterprises CEO on the state of the Presley trust and the opening of Graceland:

Jack Soden: The trust account was down to about $500,000 remaining liquid, and we spent *all* of it in the spring of '82, preparing Graceland to open. We even presold about $60,000 worth of tickets to pay some last bills before we opened on June 7. And we netted the $562,000 back in the first thirty-eight days.

Every adult needs a will. Die without one, and the state decides what happens to your property. Rarely will the state's mandate follow what you would do if you had the opportunity to act.

You have that opportunity through a will. Use it.

Action Plan

- Recognize the importance of estate planning and the urgency of doing it. Seize the day.

■ Get a good estate planner via reference from family and friends, or from your bank's trust department, or by finding out who conducts continuing legal education (CLE) at your local bar association.

■ Decide what fits you best, a will or a trust or both. Consider whom you wish to be your will's executor or the trustee of your trust. Create a living will and the two power-of-attorney documents for your dossier.

■ Designate beneficiaries for all appropriate accounts, including most of all your tax-deferred retirement accounts.

■ Communicate to all friends and family whom you're including in your plans. (Hey, *don't* communicate to those you don't—fine by us!) Include clear instructions for what these documents are, including *where* your successors can find them.

■ Be a smart heir. Sell off assets with stepped-up cost bases that you have little connection to. Redeploy the money in useful, understandable places that work best for you (not your forebear). Understand the implications for any tax-deferred accounts for which you're a designated beneficiary.

PART IV

HAVING IT ALL

Chapter Fifteen

So You're Retired Already, Eh?

There's no fool like an old fool—you can't beat experience.
—JACOB BRAUDE

CONGRATULATIONS. YOU HAVE just lived through the worst stock market since the Great Depression!

From March 2000 through March 2003, the S&P 500 dropped over 40 percent, and the Nasdaq dropped over 60 percent. Ouch!

For those invested to the gills in stocks, those who have already completed their work lives and been living off assets previously accumulated, the payback (as opposed to payoff) has been merciless. It seems unfair, no? But recall again that risk strongly correlates with reward, and stocks as an asset mega-class are the riskiest single option. Over a long-term period, higher risk pays you higher reward. But over a short-term period, high risk can mean high losses. Voilà.

Lots of books talk about how to invest for retirement. Few, it seems, provide anything on investing *within* retirement, which is the aim of this chapter. As you guessed from our title, this chapter is dedicated to those who have already left the workforce. We hope you've had a great life so far and intend to continue having a great one. That is truly having it all, which is why we kick off our "Having It All" section by speaking to you.

Oh, and on a side note, we began the book by asking in Chapter 1, "Why Retire?" One may be forgiven for wondering why we then go on to title this chapter "So You're Retired Already, Eh?" We had said, in effect, "Never do so!"

Well, all of our previous thinking still applies, okay? We've occasionally had to use the "R" word for convenience, but we do so reluctantly. Let's make it clear that here we're speaking primarily to those who are no longer deriving any meaningful salaried or part-time income.

But never really *retire,* okay?

FOR FURTHER THINKING

Charles Barkley on life after retirement:

Tom: You know, Charles, we hear a lot about athletes whose lives, when their career ends, lose a little bit of polish, a little bit of fun. What has your life been like since the end of your NBA career?

Charles Barkley: It is weird, because when you finish playing, you have to take a good hard look at yourself in the mirror. One of the people I wrote about in my book is Magic Johnson. As much as I liked him as a basketball player, the stuff he is doing for these inner cities across the country makes me love him even more as a person. I don't know if people know the stuff he is doing. These inner cities where he has built buildings—Starbucks, Borders, movie theaters, and huge shopping malls in the middle of these inner cities. People are moving in, and other businesses are moving in. You see this all around the country, and it has been phenomenal.

One of the things I talked about is, I can make a decision what I want to do with my life. Did I just want to be rich and famous when it was over and have a lot of money? I said no. The first thing I did was give my high school a million dollars so underprivileged kids could go to college. Then I gave my college a million dollars to attract poor kids. Then I gave another school a million dollars. I think the poor kids deserve an opportunity to be successful.

YOUR 60/40 ASSETS AND
YOUR 4.2 PERCENT WITHDRAWAL RATE

The simplest way to determine how long your money will last you is to identify three key variables: (1) how much you have; (2) how much you spend; and, most important, (3) the percentage of what you spend compared to what you have.

A fourth key variable enters into the equation, but it's not nearly as controllable or predictable. That's how long you'll live. Because most of us are not in a position to answer the question with real precision, and since we'd probably prefer to think about *life* more than *death*, let's stay focused on numbers one through three.

First, how much you have. This isn't a number that you can change very easily at the moment. What you have is what you have. We'll try to help you preserve it, or even get more of it, but you don't have any direct control over the present amount.

Second, how much you spend. You enjoy a great deal of power over how much you spend. Virtually every dollar you spend is a choice you've made. Even the traditional so-called nondiscretionary spending—for instance, mortgage payments—involve choice. As we made clear in Chapter 8, moving into less demanding, less expensive domestic circumstances is something you definitely have control over, and it's often a great idea.

Now that we've briefly considered how much you have and how much you spend, we arrive at the key statistic: the ratio between the two, or "withdrawal rate." The withdrawal rate is ideally something that every concerned retiree understands, tracks, and alters as necessary.

For example: Let's say you are a couple with total assets of $800,000, spending $33,600 a year. You are also getting Social Security of, say, $17,000 for your overall income of about $50,000. You find that $50,000 allows you to live comfortably, and you can even reinvest some of that if you tighten your belt. What's your withdrawal rate?

If we take your annual nest-egg drawdown of $33,600 and divide it into $800,000, we find that you're annually spending 4.2 percent of your invested assets. That 4.2 percent is your *annual withdrawal rate.*

And you know what? For a hypothetical retirement period lasting twenty years, a withdrawal rate of 4.2 percent is pretty much optimal, according to recent sources we use.

Why is that? Why is there an optimal withdrawal rate at all, and why would it be 4.2 percent?

The assumption is, first of all, *an optimal mix of 60 percent equities and 40 percent fixed income.* This mix has been rigorously back-tested by John Greaney, maintainer of the Internet's Retire Early home page (www.retireearlyhomepage.com), and a host of our Retire Early home-page discussion board at Fool.com. That mix over a twenty-year period keeps the majority of your assets in a better performance bracket, enabling your money to grow beyond inflation over two decades. But a full 40 percent is socked away, generating pure income, giving you a defense against bad markets and a steady stream of income (together with dividends from your stocks).

Let's boldface those two key general guidelines: **For those planning on twenty years of retirement, tend to invest assets 60 percent in stocks and 40 percent in fixed income, and shoot for an optimum maximum withdrawal rate of 4.2 percent.**

Using a century's worth of data to examine every single real-world twenty-year increment, John Greaney has undertaken to figure out the highest withdrawal rate you can use and still wind up with guaranteed funds twenty years later. That figure is, again, about 4.2 percent. Here's some good news: Among all possible historic twenty-year periods, at a 4.2 percent withdrawal rate the median amount of money you wound up with, twenty years later, is about 70 percent *more* than you started with.

Once more we're talking optimal. If you want to take some risks and withdraw 5 percent of your funds, in most periods of history you will have money left over after twenty years. You can even gamble with 6 or 7 percent withdrawal rates, though note that we use the word "gamble." The longer you live, the more likely you are to have increasing amounts of money left over, thanks to the power of compounding.

Another way of expressing that 4.2 percent is to turn it around and show its equivalence in the years of savings that you need in order to generate enough income for your expenses. So if you take the reciprocal of .042 (remember this from math class with Mr. Wales?: Just divide .042 into one), you'll come up with 23.8.

What does 23.8 indicate?

Simply that whatever you calculate your annual expenses to be in retirement—and assuming you'll spend the same amount each year—multiplied by 23.8 equals the total assets needed to ensure that you can live comfortably, and probably indefinitely funded, in retirement.

Example time. Say you are a widow living in a state with a low cost of living, and you project spending $21,000 annually in retirement. Multiply that by 23.8, and you wind up needing $499,800 (or basically $500,000) saved and invested—60/40 in equities and fixed income—over the next twenty years and beyond. This does account for inflation, by the way.

We've been good at giving you news throughout this book, though a fair amount of it has been bad. Well, here are two bits of good news.

First, we tend to spend less as we grow older. This need not indicate that we're having any less fun; it's that we don't get around as much anymore! For your expense projections, this is good news and worth bearing in mind.

Second, the scenario above didn't include Social Security. Let's alter the story slightly. You've determined that $21,000 is about what you will spend per year. However, you get $5,600 in Social Security. So if you subtract that from the $21,000, you'll need just $15,400 from your investments. Multiply that by 23.8, and you reach a portfolio size of about $367,000, about a fourth less.

In all the work above, we are providing general guidelines backed by an example or two. *Everyone's situation is different.* Just as we didn't pretend to do your wills and estate planning in these humble pages, we can't possibly look at every permutation of withdrawal rate, length of time, starting asset base, etc. However, what we can do after providing you the Foolish framework for thinking through your own situation is to point you toward resources that will help you answer your own questions.

As we hope we have already made clear, the advantages of the Internet for retirees are very significant, but one of the better ones has to be the educational resources and simple interactive tools to help you make better financial decisions. Our website, Fool.com— named the number one destination on the Internet by *Barron's* for financial education—is one such example. Another site relevant to this chapter, John Greaney's Retire Early home page, mentioned earlier, has a wealth of calculators, articles, and other tools to help you figure out your situation. His site is located (where else?) at: www.retireearlyhomepage.com.

Of course, a fee-only financial planner continues to be a recommendation high on our list for those who need lots of help or coaching or both. Finally, our TMF Money Advisor service, referenced earlier and in the back of this book, can be quite helpful in this regard.

TOP CONSIDERATIONS FOR LATTER-DAY INVESTING

We just stated an optimal mix of 60 percent stocks, 40 percent bonds. Your actual mix may vary. The single biggest factor is deciding how much risk you can take (i.e., "Can I put more or less in stocks?"). Those with handsome retirement prospects can afford to keep more in stocks. Those for whom even a 15 percent drop in the value of their assets would force a severe change in living circumstances shouldn't have anything near 60 percent in stocks.

Thus, your answer on how to allocate among stocks, fixed income, and cool cash relies largely on how much you have in the first place.

We tackled the question of how to invest *for* retirement. Many of those considerations hold true for investing *during* retirement. For instance, you want to have a clear understanding of the things you're investing in. Ideally, you should have a real interest or passion in any stocks you own. You want to keep your fees down. You want to understand how your investments are performing— not just in a vacuum but in the context of how their asset class is performing overall (if your stocks are down 20 percent, you should know whether the market is also down 20 percent or down 35 percent, or up 10 percent over the same period). Context, context, context.

Motley Fool member Don Bell is comfortably retired. He knows where his money's coming from, how much he has, whether it's enough, and if it will last indefinitely. Has Don made all the right moves? "Unfortunately, my financial planner didn't tell me much of what I've learned—or I wasn't listening—so the price of my education was a few hundred thousand dollars."

Despite the setback, how did he do it and what has he learned? Here are a few tips that we include because we agree with him.

First and most important, know what you're doing. "You should be able to explain to anyone you know how you're invested." And *why*. If you can't defend your choices under skeptical questioning with confidence and reason, you are not where you need to be. Get there by learning (a major aim of this book is to help you do so—but you already knew that).

Second, use Quicken or a spreadsheet or a yellow legal pad to get a good grasp on where your money goes. Budgeting is a waste of time if you're not tracking in a useful manner how much you spend. You'll know from this chapter and from your own daily life that knowing how much you're spending, as a percentage of how much you have (your withdrawal rate), gives you the single most useful and actionable number you need during retirement.

Third, Don has a favorite fund that comes from our favorite fund family, the Vanguard Balanced Index Fund (VBINX), "an excellent core investment for most retirees." We already mentioned this one, as you'll recall from Chapter 6. Sure enough, the fund has the following allocation as of this writing: 60 percent stocks, 39 percent bonds, 1 percent cash. Since its inception about ten years ago, the fund has had an average annualized return of 9 percent—achieved with 40 percent of its money in bonds! Its expense ratio? Just 0.22 percent over the past fiscal year.

Asset allocation, a subject we're batting about in these pages, has been thoroughly studied and turned into a Ph.D. field. One of the more knowledgeable thinkers on the subject is William Bernstein, the man behind *Efficient Frontier,* an online journal dedicated to asset allocation (at www.efficientfrontier.com). Bill also authored a book entitled *The Intelligent Asset Allocator,* which will be of interest to those who are mathematically inclined and very interested in this subject.

Bernstein underlines the importance of dividing your assets into classes whose performance does not overlap. Establishing a balance between stocks and bonds is obvious. But let's take stocks. There are growth stocks, aggressive-growth stocks, utilities, dividend-paying stocks, real estate investment trusts, etc.—all of which are called, and traded as, stocks. So "stocks" aren't *just* stocks; the term is probably too much of a grab bag.

The Bernstein school would have you balance any growth stocks and dividend-paying stocks with the aforementioned real estate investment trusts (REITs). These are essentially real estate packaged up into a company, paying you unusually high dividends based on rent flows from the properties. Thus, REITs sport typical annual dividend rates of 4 to 10 percent, and they have a pleasing likelihood of appreciating in value as well, should their properties generate higher cash flows.

You can obtain lots of great basic information about REITs and REIT investing either online or offline via NAREIT, the National Association of Real Estate Investment Trusts (located at www.nareit.com). At Fool.com, we have an outstanding discussion board about REITs, featuring savvy longtime REIT investors, including Ralph Block, who wrote the book, *Investing in REITs*. And our own Fool analyst, Mathew Emmert, covers REITs in the "Motley Fool Income Investor" newsletter.

Why REITs? Well, the high dividends should be automatically attractive to a retiree, and they generate a total average annual return rivaling that of the S&P 500. However, perhaps the biggest argument for including REITs in your latter-day investing is because their performance is highly uncorrelated with the S&P 500. That's another way of saying that REIT investors weren't bleeding with the rest of us through the market bust of 2000–2002. The Bernstein school of asset allocation reminds us that if we put 60 percent of our portfolio in growth stocks over a long-term period, we'll get a good return with some really high volatility. If we put 30 percent of our portfolio in growth stocks and 30 percent in (say) REITs, we will enjoy similarly good returns but with much less volatility and much more diversity within that stock portion, since the movement and performance of REITs are pretty sleepy and disconnected from market madness (to the upside and the down-).

To return to the important point made earlier, just because we're saying REITs are a good thing doesn't mean you should rush right out and buy them. If you're making your own financial decisions, get educated about REITs. If you have someone managing your money, don't just say, "REITs, please, Harry." Find out which REITs Harry likes and why. Either way, learn enough about these before investing in them, so you can easily explain to someone exactly why you've chosen them and why they make sense for (and to) you.

We've written at length about dividend-paying stocks, but it's worth pointing out here in particular that within that 60 percent stock allocation, much of your money should be invested in dividend-paying stocks, particularly if you need the income. REITs pay high yields but function as a separate asset class from common stocks. The best way to buy regular common stocks that pay dividends is the S&P 500 index fund, which gives you diversity with decent income.

Dividend-paying stocks harbor at least one additional advantage over normal growth stocks. Their dividends are generally secure and predictable—security and predictability being particularly comforting ideals for retirees. Companies almost always pay their announced dividends and, if anything, look to grow those over time. Thus, an equities investor can feel extra confidence in and ensure more predictability with the dividend-paying portions of stock holdings (whether index funds or individual company shares).

It is left briefly to discuss cash. Heretofore in this chapter, we have been discussing stocks versus bonds as if cash either doesn't count or shouldn't be held. Oh, but it should be. In fact, a good retiree portfolio allocation will include, as a benchmark, *two years of living expenses* in a highly liquid money-market fund. This emergency fund addresses two possible emergencies: The obvious one is a helpful cushion in the event of any bad health surprises. The not obvious one is that having this much cash stashed away enables you in some cases *not* to sell off some of your investments at bargain-basement prices after a poor market.

Which is exactly what Motley Fool member Bill was guarding against. He wrote, "If you're planning to retire early and use withdrawals from an IRA or other retirement plan as your main income, be sure you have substantial assets outside your plan to cover shortfalls. When I retired, I expected the growth of my SEP-IRA to exceed my cash needs by the third year. Instead, with the drop in market value, my SEP is about 20 percent less this year than in the first year. Fortunately, I have good investments outside the retirement plan to make up the difference."

That really beats the heck out of selling your stocks at the bottom. As financial columnist Scott Burns puts it, if you're having to withdraw from an equity-based plan at the bottom of a bear market, that's functioning like dollar-cost average in reverse: "You are always selling *more* shares when prices are down than when they are up." One such victim of this, Fool member Russ MacDonald, had to sell off his stocks at depressed prices and then go back to work. "I am much less trusting now of my future portfolio performance. I want to make sure that I never come even close to the 'safe' withdrawal rates as published (around 4 percent per year). My goal is to never withdraw more than 2.5 percent of my portfolio in any one year. If this means I need to work, like right now, then so be it. It is far more important to feel good about your financial situation than to be constantly worrying."

For some, the surprise is that you can live on quite a bit less income after retirement, due mainly to the fact that you stop saving and stop contributing to Social Security. Of course, for many, this is offset by increased medical insurance costs.

"GUYS, I DON'T HAVE ENOUGH!"

You know the general level of optimum withdrawal rate. You also know that the number isn't chiseled in stone. The richer will withdraw less; the poorer may have to settle for withdrawing more.

Anyway, given that this chapter is primarily for those already in retirement, we'll hope our subsection title doesn't express your predicament. But we understand it might. So herewith are some of our best ideas to help you put yourself in the path of prosperity.

Live Better, Spend Less

As we said earlier, you can't control your present level of assets, but *you can control your future expenses.* That means starting now, today, in the next hour, this minute. This theme of expense control runs through all our previous books, and probably will through all our future ones.

Speaking of "How much do I need to retire?" and calculating withdrawal rates, AARP provides this helpful parameter: "A rough rule of thumb: For each $50 reduction in your planned monthly retirement budget, you will need about $10,000 less in your total nest egg (assuming a 7.75 percent annual return over 30 years)."

But we're not here to tell you to spend less. Other books can do that. Why don't we like that? Because the concept of cutting back because you're supposed to, or have to, is always unnecessarily painful and off-putting. A much better approach is a focus on better living. *Ask how you can improve the way you live, and recognize the specific ways that would save you money.*

Quitting smoking is probably the ultimate example. Not only do you extend your life, perhaps significantly, but you also save *so much money* as a result. If you need some help quitting, visit http://quitsmoking.fool.com. We have other aspects of day-to-day living that are similarly expensive in more than one way (money, health, etc.). And in our consumer bonanza of a society, you have all sorts of replacement products that offer you a similar quality of life at a lower cost. Buy generic—it's the same stuff! Have a friend over and brew your own coffee instead of driving (costing you gas) to spend three times as much surrounded by strangers at Starbucks. Walk or ride a bike—don't drive—you'll enjoy the fresh air and benefit from the exercise. Learn a new game online, like bridge or hearts, at a free site like Microsoft's Games (www.zone.com). That's certainly cheaper, more social, and more challenging to the mind than repeat payments to your local video rental store or pay-per-view channel. The list goes on and on.

Motley Fool member Pat took up a brand-new hobby in retirement: wood carving. "I like the creative or artistic bent that it requires. It also provides rapid gratification or critical feedback." Pat had retired from software design and communications-system engineering, which involved "lots of numbers, lots of technical jargon and analysis."

Why wood carving? "There are many aspects to this craft. You can carve 'in the round,' or figures. You can chip-carve and make just patterns or Pennsylvania Dutch hex signs. Or you can carve in relief, which creates a picture in the depth of three quarters of an inch. . . . Some of the objects turn out better than others, but all of them teach me something."

Expressing ourselves through craft, especially if we didn't tend to do so during our work lives, reminds us of how many wonderful challenges and opportunities life presents. It is also a great way to while away the hours without spending inordinate amounts of money to "pass the time." Pat's experience makes us wish that any of our four grandparents, who have all departed this world, had taken up some craft in their latter years. We would treasure any keepsake or gift they had left us as a result of their creation. Hey, wait—come to think of it, our grandmother knitted us enchanting velvet Christmas stockings that we still happily hang over the mantel today. (As we only see them at Christmas, we tend to forget.)

So notice that our emphasis isn't on saving money for saving money's sake. Whether you quit smoking, bike more and drive less, or take up a new craft, the emphasis is on *living better*, enjoying yourself more, and spending less.

Here's the key: Living better and saving money don't have to compete against each other—in so many ways, they can conspire together.

Get in on the conspiracy.

MOVE SOMEPLACE CHEAPER

If you own a home, you can quickly generate more assets for retirement by selling it and finding a cheaper dwelling. We covered this in Chapter 8. But just to review, those living on either coast are usually in areas with a high cost of living and high real estate prices relative to those in the interior or the South. If you and your spouse don't need all those square feet in your $200,000 house anymore, you can sell it, move, and purchase something else for $100,000—you have just gigantically added to your ready funds for retirement living. It's as simple as that.

Further, whether you're moving to the suburbs or halfway across the country, lower real estate prices also generally mean lower cost of living for everything from medical and legal fees to groceries. It's often very difficult to change our circumstances as we grow older, but living somewhere cheaper can really help you catch up on your retirement assets.

GO BACK TO WORK

That phrase may read like a bad word, but if you're saying, "Guys, I don't have enough," we're saying, "Take a hard look at this option." The job doesn't have to be full time. And prepare to see some familiar faces. Many Americans thought they would retire at the bull market's top in March 2000 and are now back in the workplace.

REGISTER TO SELL ON EBAY

Many of us accumulate collections of things over the course of our lives. Some of these collections are intentional, the work of the philatelist or numismatist. But the majority, in our experience, are unintentional. Unintentional collections are otherwise known as junk. Good news for everyone who has junk: eBay. Remember this point from earlier in the book? If you're on the Internet and point your browser at www.ebay.com, you will come across one of the most important Internet sites ever devised: a marketplace for junk. And lots of nonjunk things, too, like your coin collection. eBay is an outstanding vehicle for you to sell off things collected intentionally or unintentionally.

We don't expect if you're in a financial predicament that you'll be able to sell your way out of it. But we do suggest you think hard about items that you don't use or value (even for their sentimental value) anymore, and consider ditching them.

Hey, if you need to raise extra money, which makes more sense: (1) selling off some future income-providing investments right as they hit their trough; or (2) selling a dust-gathering collection you don't have much use for, the three sweaters you never wear, the second TV together with the second VCR?

One rhetorical question per book. There it went.

Conclusion

To sum up, you as a retiree have either achieved a low withdrawal rate and financial independence or not. If you have not, you are among a vast majority, with more constantly joining your ranks. The key for you is to adjust, and—some more *good news* (in what could be a very difficult situation)—to recognize that you still have a measure of control over *your life*.

We've introduced you to several people and their viewpoints in this chapter, each one a real retiree with real questions or answers. We presented two guys named Bill and Russ, and in closing, it's interesting to reflect more carefully on the contrast between them.

In the face of a market selloff reducing his retirement holdings, Bill has opted to curb his spending and live simpler because he loves this new phase of his life. "With the market drop, I've had to tighten my belt a bit more than I'd planned. But I'm enjoying retirement so much that I'm willing to do that rather than go back to work. Also, expensive resorts that I had always imagined I'd be regularly visiting—since I loved spending time there when I was still working—don't look nearly as inviting now that my stress level has been reduced. My priority is to enjoy the life I have, which is pretty good, really."

Russ, on the other hand, has gone back to work tenaciously. He is unwilling to risk his next quarter century on the market's whim; he intends to earn enough so that he's sitting on a pile of money, from which he aims never to extract over a hypersafe 2.5 percent.

Neither Bill nor Russ is wrong. In fact, they're both right. They have found their own answers, which suit their desires and their character. We hope we've provided enough information and perspective to help you see the best path for yourself, whatever it is.

Celebrate and recognize that you *can* take a path; it is a path open to you, and every step you take down it will improve your situation, creating success.

Action Plan

■ Estimate as best you can your annual retirement living expenses. Remember, you'll almost certainly be spending less than you do now. A general rule of thumb is that the average person usually spends only about 70 percent of what he or she was spending prior to retirement (no more need to save or pay Social Security taxes).

■ Determine your income streams (Social Security, etc.) outside your portfolio of retirement assets and subtract those from your living expenses. What remains is the amount of annual expenditure that you have to make up through your retirement assets.

■ Take the figure from number two and express it as a percentage of your retirement assets to get your withdrawal rate. Your goal is to make this equal 4.2 percent or less, which sets you up for a worry-free next twenty years.

■ Put about 60 percent of your money in stocks and 40 percent in bonds. You can establish a diversified portfolio, or just "mail it in" with the low-fee option of something like the Vanguard Balanced Index Fund.

■ If you don't feel you have enough, think hard about selling your present house, moving somewhere cheaper, and retaining the difference to add to your retirement assets. Consider taking on part-time work or making changes in your lifestyle that are focused on living better *and* more cheaply. Choose the path that makes sense for you. And acknowledge that every little effort you make improves your situation, creating success. Success is contagious.

Chapter Sixteen

Live Well

You have to stay in shape. My grandmother, she started walking five miles a day when she was sixty. She's ninety-seven today, and we don't know where the hell she is.

—Ellen DeGeneres

 You'll have trouble enjoying your financial well-being, you'll find it hard to bask in the glory of all this wonderful preparatory work you've completed, *if* you are in continuing poor health. Yes, some of our maladies are heaven-sent. They're the natural result of a brief life in a dangerous world. They can't be dieted away or walked off. However, it's a common misperception that substantially declining health is as automatic as a stone sinking in the ocean.

No, it isn't.

Of all the American generations, it will be the baby boomers who best learn the power of preventive medicine. Eating well, sleeping well, exercising regularly, and capitalizing on the oncoming load of predictive gene-based laboratory tests. A few centuries ago, they might've bled the infections out of you with leeches. You are lucky to be where you are when you are here.

We urge you then in this, the briefest of chapters, to sign up for prevention. To get ahead of your aches and pains. To defeat your poor habits (good-bye, tobacco stick). To treat your ailing digestive system with healthier foods. To get educated about your own physiology. And to be that Motley Fool member who springs up at dawn, greets the day with enthusiasm, and can find your way home after a five-mile walk!

We stake no claim to medical expertise (other than Tom's doing a decent job pulling kids' teeth in second grade), but we know enough to know that you can improve your well-being, you can make preemptive strikes on cancer, you can beat back infections and irritations with an improved diet, better sleeping habits, and an effective exercise plan. Rather than blather on here about what we've learned over the past decade of improving our own health, we offer two references:

(1) Dr. Mark Hyman's book *Ultraprevention,* an outstanding exploration into personal health, with lessons that everyone can apply in their daily lives. We recommend it to you most highly.

(2) Our lively discussion online at The Motley Fool at www. health.fool.com. You will meet thousands of others in our community, with opportunities to talk with experts about running, yoga, tai-chi, nutrition, alternative healing, and the best way to deal with your HMO.

Your financial health has been our priority here. But we're not so addle brained as to overlook the critical importance of the general quality of your life and your health and well-being. Take it on with at least equal the enthusiasm you have your financial planning, and the rewards will pile up.

Chapter Seventeen

Get a Hobby.
Get a Life.

The world's a stage on which all parts are played.
—THOMAS MIDDLETON

 WE HAVE COMMITTED the next few pages of your time to an investigation into hobbies and volunteer work. Each of these decisions has financial implications. Each can either bear fruit or yield frustration in heaping spoonfuls. This chapter is about finding the fruit.

We're talking in this section about Having It All. So let's imagine for the next few pages that you are sixty-six years old. You've stepped away from full-time work. Your kids are through college (without frequent arrest for public disturbance). You have adequate insurance. Your retirement portfolio's secure. You consider yourself in reasonably good health (courtesy of racquetball, steamed vegetables, and your beautiful spouse). And now you're looking at a train of empty squares on a calendar. Weeks of days, months of hours free from traffic to the office, stacks of paperwork, meetings, critical email, free from the singing cellular ring, *free.*

Would it surprise you to hear that all this vacant space might lead to a vacant life? You might think, in teen parlance, "Whatever!" But think about it. Take us, for example. We two have spent the last ten years of our lives rushing onto airplanes, frantically jotting notes, exiting and entering meetings, racing over to CNN, bristling at each other as only siblings can, and frankly, enjoying ourselves. But even with the thrill of all that activity, the idea of stepping into the bathrobe and slippers and morning newspaper of freedom is seductive. To shut the briefcase. Idle the laptop. Stop the mind. Sleep late, then while away a day . . . a day, a week, the end of our lives. . . .

But it's a trap.

You don't have to be "retired," and you need not interact with thousands of "retirees" online, to know that it's a trap. If you abandon schedules, halt enterprise, and close down your mind, you naturally *increase* your risk of discord, dementia, disarray, and disappointment (the four Ds; er, we just came up with them). And before you know what's happened, you'll have squandered a year at keno. Or you'll know Oprah's issue of the day better than you know *your* issue of the day. Or you'll actually rely on a phone call from your grandkids to lift your spirits (we hate to break it to you, but count on only four of those each year).

The silence of having no responsibility is a trap.

We fill our lives with plans and projects out of biological imperative. Our lives are threads of habit, and our earthly habit is industry. Undo it all at your own risk. Why take that risk when the alternative offers activity *and* ease of mind? We aren't suggesting doing for the sake of doing, or doing out of economic necessity, or doing because someone else thinks you should. Be done with all that, if you can afford to. But what about now doing the things that you love? Accepting finally who you are. Being the dream you perhaps never felt you could. To us, that means taking on your hobby as a serious endeavor, in pursuit of excellence, with unending fascination and ambition.

Your later years should be swallowed up recklessly by these passions, no matter what they are. Ice hockey. Oil painting. The National Symphony Orchestra. Cross-stitch sewing. Entrepreneurship. Antiques. Billiards. Turkish cuisine. Creative writing. Wine tasting. Political debate. Studies in child development. Bridge. Ornithology. Stock investing. Seventeenth-century African art. Whatever you choose.

We are making the bold, perhaps flawed assumption that you already know your passions. But if you don't, no matter your age (even if you're a twenty-nine-year-old) it's time to find them. That won't take much, either. Doing so now will ensure you aren't casting about anxiously for some diversion when you're seventy-three (while flipping past reruns of *Gunsmoke* and *Wheel of Fortune*). Not doing so will increase the probabilities that you'll live declining years. That your best days are finished. That your final decades were a departure from vitality and vigor. That you did *retire*.

So how do you find your interest after decades of fulfilling obligations?

Start by listing them with abandon. Everything counts. If you love films, note that. If you love crossword puzzles, that, too. Mapmaking. Evening walks. World War I history. List them. Then commit a solid week of all your creative energy, enthusiasm—all of yourself—to each interest individually. Go at them one by one (you might frighten your spouse with some of these, so restrain yourself as needed). Find out if they taste like chocolate, dart like butterflies, run like an evening autumn breeze, or feel like a hole in one. Do they matter to you?

In a few weeks, or a month or two at most, you'll know which are the pretenders and which are genuine, enduring fascinations. At that point it's time to throw yourself into the arms of each survivor. Time to make little worlds out of them. How? Here's our six-step process.

(1) GOOGLE IT

Buy a notebook for each of your true interests. Then sign on to the Internet. Tap over to www.google.com and search your interest online. You'll find articles, interviews, photographs, book references, and buzzing communities—a whirl of activity around your interest. That goes for oil painting, chess, silent films, helicopter skiing, astronomy, perfecting your game of squash, investing in stocks, travel in sub-Saharan Africa, the senior Olympics, etc., a million times over.

Read and mark in your notebook every interesting thing you learn: of particular importance, the titles of any books cited. Now let your mind race into daydreams (you're conducting the Washington Symphony Orchestra; you're bowling for the city championship; your paintings line the walls of the most elegant French restaurant in town).

(2) AMAZON IT

Now float over to www.amazon.com and type in every interesting book title you've come across. Search books with similar titles, and read the editorial and customer reviews. Then be reckless in buying. You're investing in your future endeavor. Let the capital expenditures run high. Buy ten books on ice sailing if they look promising. We've read books about business and investing exhaustively for years. Don't let your hobbies go underresearched or underdeveloped.

When the books arrive, read them on rotation, and keep ongoing notes in your notebook.

(3) JOIN A CLUB OR COMMUNITY

You should either join (or start) a social club or online community tied to each of your interests. The Motley Fool Community (www.boards.fool.com) costs a few bucks a month and features discussions between the intellectually curious (among them, two Foolish brothers) on everything from money management to travel to golf to board games to exercise and nutrition and more. You can join or start any discussion group in Fooldom. Take a free monthlong trial and come for a visit.

In your nearby urban area, social clubs exist for just about anything you can imagine. If your interest isn't shared socially, or if you don't want to hang with people you don't know, then start your own club. Get your friends involved. Backgammon? Have twenty guests over for a weekend round-robin tournament next month. Rotate houses. Keep statistics. Take in contributions from players and dole out rewards to the year-end winners.

There is no excuse for not having an active social outlet for your interests.

(4) MEASURE YOUR SUCCESS

Pursue the first three steps, and you'll find that your hobbies are occupying more and more of your creative energy. Now it's time to keep score. We're not suggesting that you take an intensely competitive perspective, but you should pursue mastery. Write the best mystery books you can. Become Houston's foremost expert on the Tudor reign in England. Get your golf handicap below 15, then 10, then 5.

Track your performance daily. Set specific expectations and goals. Then beat them. You're experienced enough to be the greatest coach you've ever had, the one who sets standards, demands excellence, and cheers you on unconditionally. Settle for nothing less in the pursuit of your dreams.

===

FOR FURTHER THINKING

Cassandra "Elvira, Mistress of the Dark" Peterson's smartest investment:

Cassandra Peterson: Well, it was partly accidental and partly because my husband is very knowledgeable in these things. He took every single drop of our money, which was a considerable sum, out of the stock market in the summer of 2000.

David and Tom: Wow.

Peterson: It was just the greatest timing, and that is the money we used [to make our own movie].

David: Do you consider that—does *he* consider that—lucky timing, or was he doing a lot of work and he just felt things weren't . . . and also, *why* didn't he send us an email?

Peterson: *(Laughter)*. It was so lucky . . . Meanwhile, he is telling his dad he ought to take out his money. His dad leaves his money there, and it tanks. But we took the money out because we decided to make [our own] movie, and it was just lucky. So we will see if that is our smartest move, but I think it is going to be. We definitely have covered our tushies so far. We have made the money back for the film, and now [the rest] is all going to be bread and butter.

═══════════════════════════════════════

(5) LOOK FOR INCOME

Perhaps at some point in this chapter, you have thought, "What is all this? This seems silly. My life's fine as it is." But let's make this clear: We're trying to make it better. Take our suggested steps of (1) narrowing your list of interests to the essential few; (2) voraciously reading about each; (3) attaching a social outlet to each; and (4) measuring your performance. We are betting that your life will fly even higher than it is today. Take our bet. See what comes of it.

If you've completed the steps and you could use more income, step five is to look for commercial applications. The majority of hobbies have some business outlet. If you love movies, write reviews for a local paper or magazine. If you love investing in stocks, consider registering to provide professional counsel to friends and family. If you have a luxurious garden, offer consulting services through your local nursery.

If that sounds like a nuisance and you don't need the money, skip it. But if you're among those who could use a little income and are tired of dancing when the boss yells "Dance," set up your own modest venture. Who knows where it will take you.

(6) TEACH IT

Often the most logical, most rewarding, and most valued outcome of the pursuit of your passions is an opportunity to be the Zen master. To be Yoda. To instruct your peers or, ideally, we think, younger people. You've seen the statistics. There are 275 million Americans. Seventy-five million of them can be classified as boomers. Guess what? There are more than 100 million people in America younger than you who are looking for guidance in life.

Your generation has the size and momentum to change the feel of our free society in untold ways. How about to improve the lives of young people? It must be evident that the more attention, instruction, and love that young people under the age of twenty-five get, the more they flourish. The more involved they feel, the more productive they are, then the larger the stake they have in opportunity, freedom, a rich culture, and peace.

Conclusion

No need for a lengthy conclusion. Invest in your hobbies. Begin to make them your second and third careers. Why wait another day?

Action Plan

■ Grab your retirement-planning notebook and make a new list—of your interests. Include everything from current hobbies to topics that have always fascinated you but you've never explored very much. Include activities, places, subjects, and people you enjoy spending time with. Examples: tennis, bird-watching, painting, children, kayaking, traveling, Japanese drumming, Guatemalan culture, Indian cuisine, Haitian art, Appalachian music, geology, wine making, cheese tasting, the French language, the elderly, photography, board games, puzzles, gardening, nutrition, genealogy, local politics, community theater, martial arts, golf, guitar, and so on.

■ Research and learn more about a bunch of these interests, perhaps your top five or ten. Learn what you need to know to become involved, and discover what resources are out there.

■ Begin participating in some of these activities and interests. Join a club or a group of people who share your interest, or find some of these people and form a new club or group.

Chapter Eighteen

Volunteering

Wherever life takes us, there are always moments of wonder.
—FORMER PRESIDENT JIMMY CARTER

 YOU MAY HAVE or you may not have loved him as the peanut-farming thirty-ninth president of the United States. Some cite peace in the Middle East. Some cry gas lines. Some applaud the narrower gap between rich and poor. Others recall hyperinflation—or worse, *stagflation*. Regardless, few dispute that Nobel Peace Prize recipient Jimmy Carter is among the more admired Americans today.

Carter has spent the last two decades volunteering as a negotiator for international peace and as a monitor of foreign political elections. He builds houses one week out of each year with Habitat for Humanity. And he fights hunger, disease, and poverty through the Carter Center at Emory University in Atlanta, Georgia. He's an intellectually driven caped crusader of sorts.

Yet does anyone think President Carter volunteers merely out of a sense of obligation? He hasn't thrown himself frowningly into the service of others because he *should*. He does it—perhaps just like you do—because he *enjoys* the work, believes in its aims, and loves the results.

Guess what? We Fools don't think you should sign up for volunteer work out of mere obligation. If the work doesn't reflect your natural interests, you'll burn out quickly enough. You shouldn't be grumpy as you drive into the free medical clinic. You shouldn't be annoyed to count cans of food. Honestly, how much help can any of us offer if it's assistance we dread giving?

The best volunteer work will never be about mere "duty," one's "debt to society," the commitment to the "greater good." It is *not* something that should be required of young people, old people, or anyone. Volunteer work should be your voluntary decision to help others. The work should be rewarding. It should exercise your abilities. It should matter to you. If it does, you'll make it a sustainable part of your life.

What you may not know is that there are endless opportunities to volunteer small or large amounts of your time and energy and talent for the causes you believe in. Here's how we'd suggest going at it.

FIND WORK THAT YOU LOVE

Your search for volunteer community work should resemble a job search. True, you won't be angling for a salary and the prospects of a whopping bonus. You've counted in cash long enough. But you will operate off a scoring system. Your volunteer scoring system counts in units of satisfaction, spirit, camaraderie, advocacy of your beliefs, and service to others. Please don't think that any old volunteer work will score high for you. Think how often, in a rush to do good, many get involved in activities that aren't interesting to them, aren't sustainable, and simply aren't right. Don't dive into volunteer work any more than you would have into a career. If you search around a little, you'll be overwhelmed with great opportunities.

You could become a volunteer park ranger in the wilderness; a volunteer board member at a growing local business; a volunteer firefighter; a volunteer assistant math teacher in college; a volunteer piano instructor; a volunteer librarian; a volunteer soccer coach; a volunteer hospice-care worker; a volunteer guidance counselor; a volunteer chef. You are limited only by your imaginative ability to help others. The simple questions volunteer workers sometimes forget to ask are:

What do I love to do?

How, through that talent, can I help others?

Ask them of yourself before getting involved in any organization.

FIND A GROUP YOU UNDERSTAND AND BELIEVE IN

Once you've listed your interests, begin looking for relevant organizations. They're out there. If you want to work with children, consider the local schools, the Boys & Girls Clubs of America, summer camps, and churches. If you want to work outdoors, check around for state and local parks, wilderness preserves, public gardens, and outdoor leadership programs. If you speak perfect French and love the language, contact high schools, universities, and local language programs to determine how you can help. Volunteer opportunities await virtually every human talent.

Once you've located a few different organizations, it's time to compare and contrast. First, read the mission statement of each. Second, do your best to assess how well the group executes its mission. Third, talk to both its paid employees and its volunteers. Do they sparkle with a sense of dedication? Do they work together? Are they world-beaters? Or do they seem annoyed, ignored, or unproductive?

Remember, your volunteer work will not happen in isolation. You'll be working in a team toward a goal. Before signing up, make certain you believe in the people tasked with carrying forward the mission.

ENSURE THERE IS IMPORTANT WORK TO BE DONE

How does stuffing envelopes sound? How 'bout selling raffle tickets? Answering phones? Organizing files all day? What about making repeated phone calls, asking potential donors for money?

Wherever we work, whoever we are, we'll eventually be asked to participate in the little agonies of life. There's no avoiding them altogether. But plan to get more out of your volunteer work than these little agonies. Any organization that would stick you, our cherished Fool, with sorting and calling and filing and grunting exclusively is not worth your time. Demand a place that needs your hands-on expertise.

After all, you'll be forgoing cash compensation in lieu of what? Stamp licking? Telemarketing? Paper shuffling? Yes, some of that, sure. You want to help. You believe in the mission. But you'd like to do far more. If you plan to volunteer at a hospice, you'd like to get the training that will allow you to work directly with the patients and their families. Yes, you'll clean up the kitchen when needed. Yes, you'll deposit the donation checks at the local bank. But your talents will go wasted if your time is reduced to these menial (albeit valuable) tasks.

How can you find out what the volunteer experience is like at, say, your local food bank? Drop by and ask the volunteers directly. Make sure there's a need for you to perform important work. If not, keep looking.

MAKE NO SIGNIFICANT UP-FRONT COMMITMENT

Once you've found a perfect place to work, stop. That might sound churlish and cold of us. Darned Fools. But think about it. Take on too much up front, and you'll burn out, contribute inconsistently, and end up hurting the organization you wanted to help. How? They'll have invested time in training and scheduling you. You'll overcommit, then pull out altogether when they're most relying on you, and you'll prove a disappointment to the very people you wanted to help.

Your best strategy is to start small.

Ask for a one-week trial, then commit to a day of service each month. If, at the outset, you only touch your toe in the shallow end of the labor, you won't really be missed if the work isn't for you. You won't find yourself sitting on the other side of a desk resigning, hemming and hawing about, oh, how your daughter needs you at Chuck E. Cheese's with the grandkids every Thursday, and how your arthritis has been acting up, and how you don't have the time you thought you did.

Don't put yourself in a position to make excuses. Instead, start small. Let your enthusiasm build. You might be surprised by where you are in six months. Your volunteer work may have become full-time assistance at Children's Hospital, or a life of wild-life caretaking in Glacier National Park in Montana, or twenty hours a week of educated tour-guiding at Boston's Gardner Museum.

FOR FURTHER THINKING

George Foreman on the Grill:

Tom: Do you think you've made more money from your boxing career or from sales of the George Foreman Grill?
Foreman: No doubt, the grill has been more successful, but it never could have happened without the boxing career, I can tell you that . . . You know, it's strange. Now, with the grill, I walk through the airport and people say, "George! I love your grill! And it works! And I have lost so much weight." I hear these kinds of things, and that makes me know that success cannot be measured with money . . . because as a boxer it wasn't about the money; it was just you trying to be heavyweight champion of the world and an Olympic gold medalist.

START YOUR OWN ORGANIZATION

Once you've done voluntary work, it may be time to start your own local Carter Center. Come up with a different name, though; that's taken. Open up the _____ Center in your hometown, perhaps right out of your living room. Dedicate the group to keeping city streets clean, or to teaching troubled teens how to play chess, or to delivering turkeys each Thanksgiving.

Pick up a copy of *Managing a Nonprofit Organization in the*

Twenty-first Century, by Thomas Wolf. Getting a small nonprofit start-up off the ground won't take nearly as much work as you might suspect. You could even earn your way into our Foolanthropy year-end drive at Fool.com, taking in some extra cash to further your goals.

Conclusion

It's likely that up until you reach your sixties, you will not have been able to clear your schedule to voluntarily help others without financial reward. We understand. American life is a busy place. Our society is free and competitive. You are rewarded for working hard, but at times you face tremendous financial, emotional, and spiritual challenges. Divorce, job instability, the loss of a loved one, the collapse of an investment portfolio, the struggle to solidify a start-up business, medical problems . . . any of these may have made it impossible for you to volunteer your time. You may still not be able to, which is fine.

When you do find more time to voluntarily help others, go step by step. Before diving in, take the time to make sure you're doing what you love through an organization you believe in. That will make all the difference in an endeavor that may prove the most rewarding aspect of your life.

Action Plan

■ Do a little volunteering brainstorming. Jot down which pressing problems or areas of charitable endeavor interest you, then list your skills and talents.

■ Look over your lists and think of which organization(s) might fit well for you. A little time spent exploring online can help you discover some outfits you hadn't heard of but that might fascinate or inspire you. Click over to www.volunteermatch.org, www.idealist.org, or www.volunteersolutions.org, for example, to get matched up.

■ Choose a few of the most compelling organizations you came up with and make some calls, or drop by. Offer to lend a hand and then follow through. See how good a match each organization is.

■ Learn more about philanthropy in general and Foolanthropy in particular. Some useful websites: www.foolanthropy.com, www.give.org, and www.guidestar.org.

Chapter Nineteen

Travel

Though we travel the world over to find the beautiful, we must carry it with us or we find it not.

—Ralph Waldo Emerson

You'd think this chapter impossible. Absurd, really. How much useful travel advice can be given to more than 75 million potential readers? Some of you love the mountains, others the ocean. Some love New York City. Others dread it. Some of you have countless dollars to spend on diversions. Others are on a tight budget these days.

So our travel advice begins and ends simply.

Wake up!

Snap out of it!

Wake the heck up!

THE STAGGERING, WONDROUS, HEART-STIRRING ANNUAL WHIRLWIND ADVENTURE

You won't be able to travel forever. The trips you take over the next fifteen years of your life will create stirring experiences and lessons and great, great memories. But if you don't venture out, you don't get the lessons and memories. Worse still, if you make excursions but fail to recognize their unique significance in the eyeblink that is your life, what do you wind up with? Travel expenses, and perhaps regret.

We ask you to make a commitment now. No, we're not about to sell you a time-share! We'd like everyone who finds himself on this page—sitting wherever you are, reading the diddling notions of Fools—to forthwith sign a lifelong agreement *to take at least a ten-day trip every year for the next decade.* Scuba diving past butterfly fish off Maui. Practicing your mediocre French in Saint-Tropez. Backpacking along Coolwater Ridge in Montana's Bitterroot Wilderness area. Or sleeping late in a lower Manhattan hotel, ready to take in the beauty of J.M.W. Turner's paintings at the Frick Museum. Whatever your fancy.

The catch to our simple suggestion is that you not treat these ten-day trips as just another chance to travel. Wherever they take you, make them count. Take them on with all the ferocity you've brought to bear on your education, your career, your family, your health. Your circumstances may not allow you to travel outside of your state for ten days anytime soon. Fine, don't leave your state. William Plumer Fowler of New Hampshire, among our favorite modern poets, rarely left his home state. Though he lived past ninety, he left New England never more than a handful of times. The great ocean, New England's marshes and blue herons, and the sunsets over his cross-country skiing were more than enough to shake his senses and rattle awake his spirit.

It hardly matters where you go. But, from our Foolish perspective, it does entirely matter what you do when you get there. So let's get you there with a few simple financial trappings.

FIGURE WHAT YOU CAN AFFORD

Taking financial account of your travel is rudimentary. No four-dimensional spreadsheet needed. No high-paid financial advisor. Nothing but five categories. They are:

Travel costs: plane, train, automobile, whatever it'll take you to get there
Lodging: hotel, motel, bed-and-breakfast, tent, wherever you plan to sleep

Food: room service, restaurant, deli, packed meals, whatever you'll eat

Transportation: rental car, gas, taxis, buses, whatever will get you around

Entertainment: tickets to theaters, museums, parks, however you'll entertain yourself

Build your budget out of projections for each of these categories, and you will have captured your journey's primary costs. If you've never created a travel budget before, don't worry about perfect precision early on. You'll get better at this, committed as you are to taking one ten-day journey each year.

LIST OUT YOUR OBJECTIVES

Take the days, weeks, or months leading up to your trip to plan your objectives. All right, we know it sounds slightly intense. You just want to go. Why bother with goals? You're leaving precisely to get away from all the goal-setting of life. Mayhap you are tired of projects, schedules, objectives, and assessments.

We understand. But how about reducing the intensity of those other aspects of life so you might extract more pleasure from your travels? Done well, travel may sit among the top two or three activities in your life going forward. But we don't expect you'll squeeze out all the possibilities if you go off without a plan.

Are we suggesting some involved search for the deeper meaning of each little jaunt you take? Hardly. But what about a list of things you'd like to take away from the trip? Ted Leonsis, vice chairman of America Online and owner of the Washington Capitals, feared for his life aboard a troubled airliner in 1995. When he landed safely, he assembled a checklist of 101 things he wanted to do before going six feet under. That list has guided him in the half-dozen years since—one item on the list: "owning a national sports team."

You don't need to be in the wobbling cabin of a struggling commercial airliner to write out a few of your dreams. And you don't need Ted Leonsis's billion-dollar fortune to finance your desires. But do make a short list of goals for your trip. They could include:

- Parasailing
- Getting closer to a sweetheart
- Seeing the Book of Kells in Dublin
- Sleeping under the stars one night
- Running on the beach each morning
- Staying under budget for the trip
- Getting a solid eight hours of sleep each night
- Eating well, without any dishes to wash afterward
- Giving the kids a chance to see Hawaii for the first time
- Bringing the handicap down on the links
- Walking the streets of Moscow past midnight (probably not the best idea)
- Practicing Swedish

Check off each item as you achieve it.

FOR FURTHER THINKING

WD-40 CEO Gary Ridge on the strangest use of WD-40:

Gary Ridge: In Hong Kong some time ago there was a python snake caught in the suspension of a public bus, and they used WD-40 to get that little slippery guy out of there.

KEEP A RECORD

Unless you have a dramatically better memory than we do (and you might), you're liable to forget much of your trip within six months. Take the video camera, digital camera, or just a good ole pen and notebook and document your journey. Your grandchildren will soak this stuff up. You might even enjoy sifting through some of it when you're nodding off in a rocking chair three decades hence.

By taking account of your trip, you will automatically intensify the experience. You won't let yourself watch *Oprah* on a Tuesday afternoon in Rome. You'll note the painters you loved at the Museum of Fine Arts in Montreal. You'll have actual video evidence of your birdie on the seventh hole at St. Andrews. Keep a record of your trip, and you'll take even more steps to making it count.

Conclusion

We've written this chapter and the few preceding it because we don't believe you can Have It All unless you look beyond good financial decisions to make good *life* decisions. Those include—among much else—health, engagement in the world around you, and travel.

Foolishness, to us, means resisting the conventional Wisdom of the world around you, a world telling you to "retire," a world that often makes thoughtlessness or numbness convenient and almost soothing alternatives to their active opposites: the exercise of intellectual curiosity, and the zest and sensuousness of exploring the world. We focused here on a few simple travel tips Motley Fool–style, because travel is such wonderful and enriching recreation. No wonder so many older people we know travel ten times more than they did when they were our age. "Recreation" is for us to re-create, which is what we can do and almost naturally do when we change environments and cultures. Re-creation is a key part of Having It All.

If you're willing to take us up on the idea of making an annual commitment to a trip of at least ten days' duration, all you'll need is a simple budget, a list of objectives, and a device for recording. Stay close to your expense projections, check off more than half the items on your list, and come home with a few glimpses of the way it was, and you'll have formed the habit for taking a staggering, heart-stirring, annual whirlwind adventure.

Action Plan

■ Make a list of things you want to do in your lifetime. Then start tackling each of those things one by one. You might be surprised at how many you can accomplish with a little planning.

■ Next, daydream about trips you'd like to take. These can be to places near or far. Include some pipe-dream voyages, too.

■ Figure out how much your dream trips would cost. Then price each trip more aggressively, coming up with low-cost options such as less fancy lodging, discount airfare, etc. Some places you've longed to visit might be more affordable than you think.

■ Now *go* on one or more of these trips! Take a camera with you (perhaps a video recorder, too) and record your journey. Also keep a journal in which you detail what you did each day and what your impressions were. These trip journals can become family keepsakes.

Chapter Twenty

Focus on What You Can Control

Whether you think you can or whether you think you can't, you're right.

—HENRY FORD

 NO ONE'S LATTER years are perfect, just as no life is perfect and no relationship is perfect. But if you're finding by book's end that you will Have Enough or Have More Than Enough or even Have It All, wonderful!

Most of us are just shooting for having enough.

So if you're going to have it all, marvelous! This final quick thought is primarily directed to those . . .

. . . who may not or do not think . . .

. . . after reaching this point in the book . . .

. . . that they *will* have enough.

We cannot guarantee anyone happy and safe decades at the end of his life. But what we *can* do, and what we've tried hard to do in this book, is to help you make better decisions about your money.

FOR FURTHER THINKING

The late Mister Rogers on greed:

David: What do you think it is that drives people to want far more than they could ever use or need?
Fred Rogers: I frankly think it is insecurity. How do we let the world know that the trappings of this life are not the things that are ultimately important for being accepted?

Even using good advice, you still can't control important aspects of your financial life. For instance, you may be forty-eight, in debt, and only beginning to realize the importance of saving. You have no way to get those forty-eight years back. Your age—the more limited amount of time you have to make things right, the limits that you face on long-term compounded returns—is the greatest factor working against you. And it's one you can't control.

Or you may have watched your stock portfolio lose 40 percent of its value at the golden age of seventy. Can you control the market? Make it go back up again? Neither can we. The closest thing we have to controlling it is timing it—trading in and out on the presumption that we know where it's headed. We think timing the market successfully is about as much of a will-o'-the-wisp as controlling its movements.

FOR FURTHER THINKING

Twenty years of growing profits later, Whole Foods Market CEO John Mackey on overcoming adversity:

We opened the first Whole Foods Market in 1980. We had a flood after eight months of being open—the worst flood Austin had had in a hundred years—and we were eight feet underwater. We were out of business in the first year, but fortunately, we were able to rebuild and get open thirty days after that flood. That was an impetus for expanding to a second store . . . to get out of the flood zone.

Of course, it's frustrating to accept that we can't smooth out the market's returns or push them higher. Nor have humans invented a technology to reverse our age. So let's forget about the things we can't control. Let's concentrate instead on what we can control:

Your decision making. Your focus. Your discipline. And your *attitude*. Your attitude, as much as any other attribute, on its own will help to create or unravel prosperity in your latter decades—prosperity of body, mind, spirit, and bank account.

Do you have power over your activities in the next twenty-four hours?

You betcha. Over the next twenty-four hours, you have the power to spend less, earn more, save more, look for new or better opportunities, and ensure your investment portfolio is both comprehensible to you and well allocated. You have the twenty-four hours after that, too. And so on.

You could make the next year of your life the single greatest. You could do things that others will look back on and say, "Wow! He really showed us something there," or "What a woman! That was the year she set the rest of us up—I've never seen anything like it."

You may be thinking that you don't have enough. But how about *doing something* that will help ensure you do have enough? No harm in trying. Indeed, so many things to gain in trying! And your own disciplined efforts to help yourself—driven by your good attitude—will make it more and more likely that others will be inspired to help you along, if and when you need it.

FOR FURTHER THINKING

George Foreman on yet another comeback:

Tom: Okay. Buy, sell, or hold the idea of another boxing comeback for George Foreman?
George Foreman: Buy. If I get broke, I am coming back.

As it is with planning your next decade or three, so, too, with so many other aspects of our lives: Success is earned; it doesn't just happen. The gratification that comes from earning it is intense. And the surest way to it is to understand which things you can control and to focus your efforts there. Reminds us of the Serenity Prayer, which comes in many different forms, one of which we want to leave you with.

> Dear God, help me find the strength to change what I can change, the courage to accept what I cannot change, and the Foolishness to tell the difference.

Action Plan

■ Here's a great exercise we first encountered in a college class: Write your own obituary. Make it reflect the kind of life you hope to have lived by the time you reach the big harp academy in the sky. Then spend some time thinking about steps you can take to live that life. You might not achieve everything, but you can boost the satisfaction rating you end up giving your life.

■ Think back to all the action plans in this book—one for each chapter. Vow to take at least one step from one of them by tomorrow. Put your money where your vow is, and place a $5 or $10 bill on your kitchen table as a reward. Once you complete one step, buy yourself a little something nice. (Or sock it away in your retirement fund.)

■ Plan to work through all the action plans over the next six months. If you aim to do them all within one month, you'll likely burn out. Take it somewhat easy—perhaps tackle one chapter and plan per week.

■ When you're done, lend this book to a friend or relative to help him or her secure a more comfortable and enjoyable retirement.

Acknowledgments

 IN YOUR HANDS you hold not only the musings of two brothers but the collective effort of many similarly Foolish people, whom this page exists to thank.

First, we thank our family and friends who supplied us both encouragement and, necessarily, overlarge cups of coffee that kept us writing into the wee hours. Lucubration, baby, it's a way of life. Within our family, we'd particularly like to point up the special efforts of super lawyers Bill Curtin and Helen Bragg Curtin Cleary for their advice on wills and estates. Our only regret: They went to Duke. But they're living proof that Duke graduates can contribute meaningfully to society, as well.

Hearty applause goes to our crack team of writers, editors, and radio producers at Fool HQ. In particular, we put our hands together for Robert Brokamp, Selena Maranjian, and Dayana Yochim, whose expertise breathes through select chapters of this book. They know how overrated we are—sssshhhhhhhhhhhhhhh! Our broadcasting team of Greer and Broido did a great job listening back through past Motley Fool radio shows, enabling us to inject our book with Foolish quotations from a highly motley selection of celebrity guests. And to David Braze, Wendy Goldberg,

Russ MacDonald, Cathy Giunta, and AARP we say *merci beaucoup* for consulting and reviewing *The Motley Fool's Money After 40* in progress, ensuring that we covered our readers' biggest concerns. And thanks to our great friend Todd Etter for his wonderful sense of humor, which frequently finds its way into this and other Motley Fool offerings.

Jonathan Mudd and Alissa Territo expertly cultivate our corporate publishing garden and once again took this book from seed to bloom. From Gardners to gardeners, thanks! Also, thanks to our longtime assistants, the overqualified dynamic duo of Reggie Santiago and Melissa Flaim.

We must also extend gratitude to our longtime agent, unacknowledged supermodel Suzanne Gluck, who is almost, but not quite yet, unofficially in charge of New York City. And thank you as well to Mr. Simon & Mr. Schuster, neither of whom we will ever meet, but with whom we've now collaborated on a dozen or so books. These gentlemen are more than ably represented by our editor once again for this book, Doris Cooper, whose guidance and enthusiasm do credit to the world of publishing, i.e., she's pretty damn good at her job, too.

And as with all our books, we would most like to thank you, our reader, along with about 2 million other Motley Fool members worldwide. It's because of you—your own investing stories, your suggestions, and your concerns—that we continue to work hard toward solutions that will help you make better financial decisions, ultimately improving—sometimes dramatically, it is to be hoped—your quality of life. Fool On!

Additional Resources
at Fool.com

 WE HOPE YOU have enjoyed reading this book and that it has provided you with valuable and helpful information. Throughout, you have been pointed toward additional services to help you in your quest to take control of your financial destiny. Fool.com offers many of these resources at your fingertips. Consider them your Solution Centers, as they are oriented toward first educating you and then enabling you to take action. Below is an abbreviated but helpful list of some of the key areas, most of which have appeared in this book.

Insurance Center: http://insurance.fool.com
- Figure out what type you need, how much of it you should purchase, and how to get coverage at the lowest cost.

IRA Center: http://ira.fool.com
- Plan your retirement, find out if you are eligible to invest in an IRA account, which option is better—a traditional or Roth IRA—and how to open one.

Index Center: http://indexcenter.fool.com
- Learn about stock-market indices, why they are important to use in comparison to your portfolio's performance, and how you can earn their investment returns.

Retirement Center: http://www.fool.com/retirement
- Learn effective strategies for managing your retirement.

Short-Term Savings Center: http://savings.fool.com
- Determine how much cash to stash for emergencies and where to keep it.

FOOL COMMUNITY

The Fool Community is the place at Fool.com where members join together to interact, learn, question, and exchange ideas. It offers:

- Thousands of active conversations
- Staff-monitored discussions—comfortable and clean
- An opportunity to post questions and get them answered

To check out what other Fools are saying, take a peek with a thirty-day free trial at http://boards.fool.com.

TMF MONEY ADVISOR

TMF Money Advisor provides personalized, objective advice for all aspects of your financial life. With TMF Money Advisor, you get:

- Access to an unbiased, unconflicted financial advisor
- An online tool you can use to create a personal financial plan
- A collection of world-class Motley Fool seminars

To learn more about the TMF Money Advisor service and its special offers, go to: http://tmfma.fool.com.

Motley Fool Income Investor: www.incomeinvestor.fool.com
- In this monthly newsletter, Fool analyst Mathew Emmert helps you find income-producing investments to add to your portfolio. "Motley Fool Income Investor" focuses on high-yield investments, including stocks, preferred stocks, bond and muni funds, REITs, MLPs, and ETFs.

Motley Fool Stock Advisor: www.stockadvisor.fool.com
- Whether you are just starting to invest or digging deeper into analyzing stocks, Tom and David offer ideas for you in their newsletter, "Motley Fool Stock Advisor." The Gardners present their outlook on the stock market, individual stock suggestions, and tips on the best ways to manage your personal finances and investing.

Motley Fool Hidden Gems: www.hiddengems.fool.com
- In this monthly newsletter, Tom Gardner leads you in search of undervalued, overlooked small-cap stocks with strong growth possibilities and market-beating potential.

Motley Fool Rule Breakers: www.rulebreakers.fool.com
- Motley Fool cofounder David Gardner and his team search for the next big thing. This monthly newsletter guides you to finding tomorrow's landscaping-changing stocks—today.

Motley Fool Rule Your Retirement:
www.ruleyourretirement.fool.com
- Our monthly retirement newsletter, lead by Robert Brokamp, guides you to your best options in asset allocation, taxes, insurance, health-care costs, and bumping up your nest egg.

To learn more about these and other Motley Fool newsletters, visit www.newsletters.fool.com.

The Motley Fool's aim is to help you find solutions to the many and sometimes complex matters of money and investing. Whether you're looking for financial-planning assistance, research on the stocks in your portfolio, new investment ideas, information about 401(k)s and IRAs, how to save money when buying a car or home, minute-by-minute stock quotes, or a place to talk to other investors, Fool.com has all of that and more, available twenty-four hours a day.

Index

financial advisors (*cont.*)
  licensing requirements of, 67
  need for, 64–65
  professional plans of, 70–71
financial aid (college), 154, 156–57
  account owner's assets and, 154
  eligibility for, 154
  family contribution to, 154
financial independence, 8, 34, 55, 205
financial planning, 10–13
  age and, 29–30
  child-related costs in, 20–21, 29–32
  for children and college, 135–59
  credit-card management in, 40–41,
    46
  estates in, 175–89
  life expectancy in, 25
  professional plans for, 70–71
  with Quicken Financial Planner, 23
  for retirement, 17–27
  wills in, 175–76
  see also retirement, retirement
    planning
Fiorina, Carly, 142
529 plans, 146–52
  college savings plans, 146, 148–49
  prepaid tuition plans, 146, 147
flexible spending account, 97–98
foolanthropy.com, 223
Fool.com, xiv, 27, 33, 46, 130, 198
Ford, Henry, 230
Foreman, George, 6–7, 9, 55, 107–8,
    221, 232
401(k) plans, 27, 31, 34, 94, 139, 162
  minimum required distributions
    (MRD) from, 187
403(b) statement, 27
Four Quartets (Eliot), 114
Fowler, William Plumer, 225

games, 203
  retirement-savings, 34–47
Gardner, David, xi
Gardner, Tom, xi, xiv
"Gardner Consumption Theory"
    game, 38–40
Gardner Museum, 221
Gaye, Marvin, xvi
Georgetown University, 4
Getty, John Paul, 38, 40
Ginsberg, Ruth Bader, 142

Girls Club of America, 219
Giunta, Cathy, 172
google.com, 212
Gordon, Harley, 129
Graceland, 188
Greaney, John, 196
Great Depression, 36, 54, 107, 193
greed, 231
gross domestic product (GDP), 85
group insurance, 99
guidestar.org, 223
"Guide to College-Savings Plans"
    (*Business Week*), 149
Gunsmoke, 212

Habitat for Humanity, 217
Hackman, Gene, 66
half.com, 139
Hazlitt, Henry, 105
Health and Human Services
    Department, U.S., 85
health care, 20, 84–102, 208–9
  alternative medicine and, 209
  cutting costs of, 97–99
  declining employer contributions
    to, 91, 100
  hospital bills and, 98
  longer lifespans and, 87
  nutrition and, 209
  resources, 209
  rising costs of, 85–86
  spending per person on, 86
health-care proxy (medical proxy),
    124, 180
health.fool.com, 209
health insurance, xvi, 10, 202
  copayments and deductibles in, 98
  free and discounted services in, 98
health maintenance organizations
    (HMOs), 90, 98, 209
Heist, 66
Henry V (Shakespeare), xi
Hitchhiker's Guide to the Galaxy, The
    (Adams), 26, 27
hobbies, 20, 210–16
  mental health and, 211
homes, home ownership, 75–83, 204
  case study in, 79–80
  evaluation of, 76–77
  options in, 80–82
  overspending on, 75–76

About the Authors

DAVID AND TOM GARDNER cofounded The Motley Fool, an Alexandria, Virginia–based multimedia company, in 1993. They started out publishing a modest investment newsletter for friends and family, began talking stocks online in the early days of AOL, then launched their own investment education website, Fool.com, in 1997.

Tom graduated with an honors degree in English and creative writing from Brown University. David graduated as a Morehead Scholar from the University of North Carolina at Chapel Hill. With many ideas and no regrets, he quit his job writing for *Louis Rukeyser's Wall Street* newsletter in order to found The Motley Fool with his brother.

Today, The Motley Fool has grown into an international multimedia financial education company helping millions of individuals worldwide seeking to make better financial decisions and improve their overall quality of life. Tom and David have coauthored four *New York Times* business bestsellers, including *The Motley Fool Investment Guide, The Motley Fool You Have More Than You Think,* and *The Motley Fool's Rule Breakers, Rule Makers.* In addition to writing bestselling books, the Gardners oversee a nationally syndicated newspaper column, which is carried by more than 200 newspapers, and host a weekly radio program on NPR.